THE LIKENESS OF THOMAS MORE

An Iconographical Survey of Three Centuries

Frontispiece. The Frick version (3)

THE
LIKENESS OF THOMAS MORE

AN ICONOGRAPHICAL
SURVEY OF THREE CENTURIES

BY

STANLEY MORISON

EDITED AND SUPPLEMENTED

BY

NICOLAS BARKER

NEW YORK

FORDHAM UNIVERSITY PRESS

MADE AND PRINTED IN GREAT BRITAIN BY
WILLIAM CLOWES AND SONS, LIMITED, LONDON AND BECCLES

SET IN 'MONOTYPE' BEMBO

TO THE MEMORY OF
RICHARD O'SULLIVAN
1888 – 1963
A FOUNDER OF THE
THOMAS MORE SOCIETY
LONDON
1928

CONTENTS

vi

LIST OF ILLUSTRATIONS

The numbers in parentheses refer to the catalogue in Appendix A; reproductions of paintings have all been reduced, the medallions enlarged, and the prints reproduced in the same size as the original, with the exception of 38, 40 and 42 which have been reduced.

LIST OF ILLUSTRATIONS

PREFACE

'Never, perhaps, has it fallen to the lot of a human being to have his features so tortured and perverted as More's have been. At one time he is made to resemble a Turk; at another time, an Officer of the Inquisition. One artist decorates him with the robes of "Soliman The Great"; another takes care to put around him those of a mountebank or conjurer. Shaven or unshaven—with a short or a long beard—we are still told it is Sir Thomas More! In physiognomical expression he is as often made to represent the drivelling ideot, as the consequential Lord Mayor; and the immortal name of Holbein is subscribed to portraits, of which he not only never dreamt, but of which almost the meanest of his successors, in this country, might have been justly ashamed.'[1]

A first glance at the illustrations of this book might seem to offer abundant proof of the justice of this tirade. On reflection, however, it becomes clear that it ignores the significance of the two most striking facts about the portraiture of More, which distinguish its history from that of any other figure of comparable importance. The first is the abundance of portraits; if the representation of a man continues to interest a large number of people, if it is broadcast outside the limits of descendants who have a special interest in the exact reproduction of features, it will change. If, moreover, that man stands for different things to different people, as did More, scholar and chancellor, humanist and saint, the likeness will vary, as the *type* of the person depicted varies. The second fact is that the period of this survey saw the growth of the ideal of a true portrait—the man as he was, not the qualities he represented nor the office he held. At the beginning, this demand for verisimilitude was not there, and an examination of the later portraiture of More's contemporaries will shew many whose real features were permanently lost through the need to depict an idea, not reality.

If then we look again at the illustrations, it is the persistence of certain features, rather than the variation in others, which seem the more remarkable. This persistence is due, beyond doubt, to the authority of Holbein's original portraits, and the restoration of the Holbein image as the authentic likeness of More has been taken as the terminal point of this inquiry. It is a matter for some regret that it cannot here be continued further: the two statues erected in the City of London in 1880 and 1889, J. R. Herbert's romantic painting (1886) of the fallen chancellor and his beautiful daughter in the gloomy Tower, Sir Frank Brangwyn's free copy after the Windsor drawings, Eric Gill's reredos in Westminster Cathedral, and the many statues and windows in chapels and churches built in Britain and the United States and dedicated to the saint since 1935, must await separate treatment.

[1] *Utopia*, edited by the Rev. T. F. Dibdin, London, 1808, p. cxv.

On the other hand, the quantity of portraits produced during the early period, when More was not valued as he is now, is remarkable enough. The catalogue at the end of this book, incomplete as it is, reveals the strength of the memory of More and what he stood for in times when it was sometimes dangerous to speak his name and historians were silent.

The principle of this work has been to elucidate, so far as possible, the history of the Holbein likeness of More, and of the most important versions of that likeness. The author's obligations are therefore greatest to what is still the chief authority on Holbein, Arthur B. Chamberlain's *Hans Holbein the Younger* (London, 1913), which has the merit of collecting the greatest mass of information on Holbein that exists in any one work. Chamberlain's predecessors, R. N. Wornum, *Some Account of the Works of Hans Holbein* (London, 1867) and Alfred Woltmann, *Holbein und sein Zeit* (Leipzig, 1874–6), have also been useful. Among modern works we are indebted to those of Sir Karl Parker, *The Drawings of Hans Holbein in the Collection of H.M. at Windsor Castle* (London, 1945), H. A. Schmid, *Hans Holbein der jüngere* (Basel, 1948–50) and Dr Paul Ganz, *Die Handzeichnungen Hans Holbeins d. j. Kritischer Katalog* (Basel, 1937) and *The Paintings of Hans Holbein* (London, 1950); the publishers of the last, the Phaidon Press, have very kindly permitted the reproduction of one of its illustrations, which appears here as fig. 3.

Dr Ernest Weil first drew my attention to, and later obtained for me, the oblong miniature (see pp. 59–60) and merits my especial thanks. This work owes its inception to our correspondence, which began in 1944.

Mr W. M. Milliken of the Cleveland (Ohio) Museum has kindly supplied a photograph of the miniature kept there, and has given permission to reproduce it here. I am indebted to the curators of the national and municipal collections of paintings and engravings at Antwerp, Basel, Brussels, London, Madrid, New York, Paris and Versailles, and in particular to the curator of the Frick Collection, New York, who has kindly permitted the reproduction of the colour print which appears as the frontispiece. I am especially indebted to the Treasurer of Lincoln's Inn for permission to examine and reproduce the miniature in the possession of the saint's own Inn, which has recently added a fine copy of the Frick Portrait to its collection.

For biographical particulars of More thanks are due to E. E. Reynolds, *Saint Thomas More* (London, 1953) and to R. W. Chambers, *Thomas More* (London, 1935), and for bibliographical data to Frank Sullivan, *Syr Thomas More a first Bibliographical Notebook* (Los Angeles, 1953) and R. W. Gibson, *St Thomas More: a preliminary Bibliography* (Yale, 1961). The text of the letters of More and Erasmus has been derived from P. S. Allen's monumental edition of the correspondence of Erasmus, and, following Miss E. F. Rogers, whose own edition of *The Correspondence of Thomas More* (Princeton, 1947) have been most useful, references are given to Allen's text. Fr. R. F. Gardiner, S.J., of Loyola University, Los Angeles, kindly sent a microfilm of the catalogue of the Longstaff Collection of portraits of More in his care. The account of the pictorial propaganda of the Society of Jesus owes much to P. Miguel Nicolau, S.J., *Jerónimo Nadal, Obras y Doctrinas Espirituales* (Madrid, 1940). P. Nicolau's book is a doctoral dissertation presented to the University of Innsbruck, and if its typography in no measure approaches the level reached by the Spanish Jesuits, who achieved the publication of Nadal's *Evangelicae Historiae Imagines* (Antwerp, 1599), it is abundantly documented, and contains more fascinating surprises, notably his demonstration of the translation of Nadal's copper-engravings (the Wiericx brothers) into woodcuts re-designed in Chinese costume and idiom, for use in the pictorial rosary of P. da Rocha, S.J. (1565–1623).

The Portraiture of Thomas More by Hans Holbein and after: a Consultation was printed at the Cambridge University Press, and in part read to the Thomas More Society in the library of the Inner Temple on 18 October 1957. Towards this, several friends, in particular Miss O. F. Abbott (R.I.P.), Mr T. F. Burns, Mr H. G. Carter, Mrs Eric Gill, Miss P. M. Handover, Mr Alan Pryce-Jones, Mr Ronald Mansbridge, and Mr Suckling, generously assisted in various ways. This print was circulated to and criticized by various people, principally by Mr David Piper of the National Portrait Gallery, who put together a draft catalogue raisonné of portraits of More, which has not only formed the basis of Appendix A, but has been invaluable in sorting out the involved, confusing and often confused histories of the principal paintings and drawings, which my print failed to clarify. Any merit it may have lay in the fact that it attempted to relate the drawings and prints to the paintings and miniatures. Mr Piper also convinced me of the desirability from the professional standpoint of making the inquiry available to a wider public than could be reached by a print limited, as mine was, to one hundred copies.

At this point I was fortunate to obtain the services of Mr Nicolas Barker, who has been able to add considerably to the number of portraits originally known to me, notably the two medallions here described. He also found a number of early references to portraits, and in the light of these discoveries he has revised and augumented the text of the *Consultation* throughout; he is entirely responsible for the three Appendices. In this he has been materially assisted by Mr Oliver Millar, Deputy Surveyor of the Queen's Pictures, Mr J. B. Trapp of the Warburg Institute, Dr Hubertus Schülte Herbruggen, Mr J. W. Goodison, and the staffs of the Departments of Prints and Drawings and Coins and Medals at the British Museum, and of the Guildhall Library, to all of whom he wishes to express his thanks. Mr Harry Grier has kindly permitted the as yet unpublished report to the Frick Trustees to be cited, without which a crucial link in the account of the transmission of the Holbein image would be lacking.

My personal and principal thanks are due to the Thomas More Society, whose hospitality and friendship I have so often enjoyed, and especially to Richard O'Sullivan, who introduced me to the Society, and encouraged me to continue this inquiry. The dedication of this book to his memory is a small token of esteem for one whose unselfish labour over many years immensely extended secular appreciation of the character and stature of Thomas More.

Finally, it should be borne in mind that it must be a presumptuous undertaking for one without the equipment of a professional *Kunstforcher* to attempt to trace the course of the pictorial representation of any man in international fame. In the case of More, it is obviously rash indeed. Moreover, the material which has come to light in the course of this revised survey permits few positive statements about the most interesting of the problems it raises. In these circumstances I have, so far as possible, followed the prudent course of letting the facts speak for themselves; and followed, too, the original intention, namely, to extend investigation of the portraiture of More.

S. M.

July 10, 1963

Part One

HOLBEIN AND AFTER

1. INTRODUCTION

THOMAS MORE had a clear view of the value of portraiture. In the eighth chapter of *Utopia*, he describes how the Utopians set up in their market places—which were to be found 'in the myddes of every quarter' of their cities—statues of famous men and those who had deserved well of the state, in memory of their good acts and also so that the renown of their ancestors might spur and encourage posterity to virtue. Again, when his friends Erasmus and Peter Gilles sent him a diptych of their two portraits, painted by Quentin Matsys, More, while admiring the likeness, does not forget the effect of the portraits. 'Let me confess,' he wrote to Erasmus, 'I cannot suppress one passion for future fame, which tickles my vanity, whenever I recall that I shall be remembered by posterity, in letters, in books and now in pictures, as the friend of Erasmus.'[1] It is fitting then that the authentic likeness of More, the perfect example of the 'New Learning', should have been painted by Holbein, whose work had more influence perhaps than any other in introducing the art of the New Learning to northern Europe.

As More rightly saw, a good portrait can add much to a reputation with posterity. It is unlikely that the history of the portraiture of More would have demanded a survey of this nature if he had not been painted by one of the first painters of his time. It is unlikely, indeed, that any likeness with any claim to authenticity would have survived, and that, if it had, it would have overcome the tendency to depict an idea of the man, not his real features. The most important part of our purpose must be to investigate the various versions, drawings and oil-paintings, attributed to Holbein. The authenticity and if possible the priority of each must be determined, and an attempt must be made to ascertain which constitutes Holbein's own fully worked delineation of the real features of More.

These considerations occupy the first part of the work; the second will try to shew the development of the likeness of More, and to reflect the different aspects of More which brought the later portraits into existence. Erasmus said that he was not competent to describe More's many-sided character, and he knew More well; if his subtle percipience, his passion for setting down in accurate words the exact detail of appearance and mind, paused at the task, it is unlikely that we can have achieved any better knowledge. If the study of his likeness, and the reasons which demanded a likeness, have any value, it is for the light it may cast on one of the greatest men this country has produced, a scholar whose fame was the pride of the world of the New Learning, a statesman who was perhaps the last to think in terms of Christendom rather than nation, a martyr whose death marked the end of Christian unity.

[1] Erasmus: *Epistolae*, edited by P. S. Allen (Oxford, 1910–32) vol. III, no. 683. It is interesting to note that More saw the value of likeness in a portrait: 'if anyone see them', he wrote, 'he would think them moulded or carved rather than painted, they seem so to have the dimension and reality of flesh and blood'.

3

2. HANS HOLBEIN AND THOMAS MORE

ALL study of the portraiture of More begins with Hans Holbein (1497–1543). The elder Holbein in whose studio the son was trained, was an esteemed painter who practised in Augsburg, *c.* 1465–1524. Hans, now the most famous of the family, was not the only child of artistic promise; his elder brother Ambrosius was talented and, accompanied by Hans, left home between 1513 and 1514 for Basel.

Basel was an ancient see. It was founded as early as the fourth century, and during the Middle Ages its bishops took the Imperial side against the Papacy. Its situation at the junction of several trade routes gave it a commercial advantage and in the fifteenth century it had developed into an independent flourishing metropolis, dominated by an aggressive and ambitious bourgeoisie. The city's interest in the arts and sciences was encouraged during the earlier part of Holbein's stay there by the energetic patronage of the then prince-bishop, Christopher von Utenheim. Among the crafts practised in Basel, printing occupied a high place. A magnificent folio Vulgate bible printed in 1468 contributed to the renown of the city. Its printer, Berthold Ruppel, was an associate of Gutenberg, and in the half-century after the introduction of the art Basel had become the greatest typographic centre in southern Germany. Its zenith was reached in the working life of its greatest printer, Johann Froben, from 1491 to 1527. During this period he issued over 300 books, and established a reputation for the correctness of his texts and the beauty of his printing only equalled by the productions of Aldus and Junta. He employed Oecolampadius and Erasmus as readers, and among the artists who designed woodcuts for him were Urs Graf and the Holbein brothers. One of Hans's earliest commissions of this nature was the border in the form of an arch, which was first used late in 1515, and later for the dedication of the second of Froben's two editions of *Utopia* in 1518.

The early prosperity of the first years of the century did not last. The second decade was catastrophic for the Catholic religion in Germany, and, later, elsewhere. In 1517 Luther nailed his ninety-five theses on the door of the palace church at Wittenberg; in 1518 his agitation came to a head; in 1519 Eck failed to recall him to orthodoxy; in 1520 Leo X excommunicated him. In 1522 Zwingli began the Reformation in Zurich.

Within a few years the turning point came in Basel. In 1527 the prince-bishop, Utenheim, then aged, resigned the see. Before his successor, Gundelsheim, could enter the see, the bourgeoisie, moved as much, perhaps, by the future benefits to their political ambitions, their property and their pockets which they foresaw in the adoption of the German innovations as by a genuine impulse to religious reform, secured a majority on the grand council of the city and drove those faithful to the old religion to the gates. The practice of

Figure 1. The first Windsor drawing (1)

Tho: Moor Lᵈ Chancelour

Figure 2. The second Windsor drawing (2)

Figure 3. Detail of the Frick version, before cleaning

Figure 4. The Lothian version (6)

the Catholic religion was abolished in the district of Basel, the monasteries were expropriated, their lands distributed and the churches plundered. Works of ecclesiastical art and all 'graven images' fell before the axes of the iconoclasts. Thus disappeared for ever the several altar-pieces which Hans Holbein had worked at Basel since his return to the city in 1519, after a two-years' sojourn in Lucerne.

It was prudent for artists to turn—if they wished to survive—from the old saints formerly venerated to the new figures prominent in civic life. Holbein decided to seek a career as a portrait painter and during the next seven years his work became wholly secular. At the instigation of Froben, in whose house Erasmus was staying between 1521 and 1523, Holbein painted more than once the scholar more internationally famous than any other. The first version was sent to England as a present to William Warham, archbishop of Canterbury (c. 1450–1532), to whom Erasmus was indebted for many kindnesses and benefits, including the living of Aldington in Kent which he held *in absentia*. Holbein also painted a portrait and a miniature of Froben, the first probably linked as a diptych with a portrait of Erasmus. His indefinite religious position permitted him in 1523 to design the title-page and some illustrations for the Basel edition of Luther's German bible. It is improbable, however, that he, any more than Erasmus or Dürer, could sympathize with the iconoclastic element in the new religion adopted by Basel. '*Hic frigent artes*', Erasmus wrote in August 1526 from the reformed city to Gilles in Antwerp, 'Holbein is on his way to England to scrape some angels together. If he wants to visit Matsys, and you are too busy to introduce him, send your servant to show him the house.'[1] Thus the painter who had painted a double portrait of Froben and Erasmus, who was to paint More, may have met the painter who had painted the double portrait of Gilles and Erasmus, which had been sent to More.

Holbein came to London before Christmas, furnished with a letter of introduction from Erasmus to More. Though it is unlikely that they had met before, Holbein at any rate had long known of More. Both he and his brother provided decorations for the 1518 *Utopia*, although it was probably Ambrosius Holbein who drew the whole-page view of Utopia showing Vespucci's supposed companion Hythlodaye (More's equivalent for 'babbler') pointing out the island to More and Aegidius, and the delightful half-page conversation 701:7* piece showing More sitting between Hythlodaye and Aegidius under a tree in a garden, with John Clement (who was brought up in More's household, married Margaret Giggs, and later became President of the London College of Physicians) bringing them something from the house. Neither of these can be recognized as in any sense a portrait of More, but there is a superficial likeness to Hans's later portraits which suggests that Erasmus had on this occasion provided a word-portrait such as he later gave to Ulrich von Hutten.[2]

'In height and stature he is not tall, nor again noticeably short, but there is such symmetry in all his limbs as leaves nothing to be desired here. He has a fair skin, his complexion glowing rather than pale, though far from ruddy, but for a very faint rosiness shining through. His hair is a darkish

* References in the margin are to the catalogue (Appendix A) in roman type, and to the plates in italic type.

[1] Erasmus: *Epistolae*, ed. Allen, vol. VI, no. 1740.   [2] op. cit., vol. IV, no. 999.

fair, or if you will, a lightish brown, his beard scanty, his eyes bluish grey, with flecks here and there. This usually denotes a happy nature and is also thought attractive by the English, whereas we are more taken by dark eyes. It is said that no type of eyes is less subject to defects.

'His expression corresponds to his character, always showing a pleasant and friendly gaiety, and rather set in a smiling look; and, to speak honestly, better suited to merriment than to seriousness and solemnity, though far removed from silliness or buffoonery. His right shoulder seems a little higher than the left, particularly when he is walking: this is not natural to him, but due to force of habit, like many of the habits which we pick up. There is nothing to strike one in the rest of his body; only his hands are somewhat clumsy, but only when compared with the rest of his appearance.'

This was the manner of man to whom the painter was introduced. He was then 29 and More 49. Holbein could hardly have been more fortunate, or his arrival at Chelsea better timed. He was promptly commissioned to paint the members of that large household.

When he sat to Holbein, More had been a member of the king's council for nearly ten years and chancellor of the duchy of Lancaster for two. In addition, he had been the leader of many diplomatic missions, speaker of the House of Commons since 1523, and was also high steward of both universities and a principal officer of state. As early as 1506, moreover, he had won respect throughout Europe for his collaboration with Erasmus in the first of several humanist tracts; while for ten years *Utopia* had made his name everywhere famous. Known as a resolute opponent of heresy, while ardent for reform within the Church, Thomas More was England's foremost representative of what we call the 'renaissance' and his generation called the 'new learning'. Such a man was no unworthy subject for the greatest portrait painter of the age. Holbein could not fail to be moved, nor were his own and later generations unimpressed, by such a concatenation of capacities and offices, successes and honours, with the promise of still greater preferments. More was rich and could easily afford to entertain Holbein in his Chelsea house and to pay what the painter wished.

Evidently Holbein was well content to paint for him. He painted at least one large single portrait and a large canvas depicting the whole of his household. In addition, he made a number of sketches, before and after the two major paintings, among which two drawings of More and a pen and ink sketch of the family group survive. Whether the single portrait preceded the family group is not certain; but since it is convenient to begin with the largest portrait having the fullest detail, Holbein's portrait of More himself, dated 1527, is here given precedence.

3. THE SINGLE PORTRAIT IN THE FRICK COLLECTION

THE countenance depicted by Holbein during his stay at Chelsea exhibits great strength of character and largeness of mind, but it does not correspond in all respects with the description of him that Erasmus gave to von Hutten. Evidently, since 1519, More's then 'scant beard' had submitted to more frequent use of the razor, though he is not entirely clean-shaven as the detail of the face shews. The features are here set more seriously than perhaps they always were in one so renowned for quickness of wit and range of humour. But this is a formal portrait: the dignity of the subject is the first consideration. Here is More on the threshold of his highest office and that, no less, of Lord Chancellor—in which he succeeded Wolsey on 25 October 1529. England's first lay holder of that office, he now left behind him the brilliant ten years which had opened with the embassy to Bruges on the nomination of the merchant adventurers, the decade of his greatest happiness. He is shewn half-length to the right, looking right, his hands touching in front of him. He holds a folded paper in his right hand, and on his left forefinger there is a gold ring with a bloodstone set in it. He is wearing a black cap with the earflaps up, the right string hanging a little loose, and a dark gown with a rich brown fur lining turned back over the shoulders and showing at the end of the half-sleeves; the sleeves of his red velvet doublet show at the forearms. Over his shoulders is a large gold chain of SS with a clasp in the shape of a portcullis and a pendant tudor rose. His right arm rests on a stone ledge or bench end, below which the date M.D.XXVII is carved. A green curtain is draped in folds across the background, with a red drawing-cord looped across to the top right hand corner of the picture; below the gold fringe of the curtain a glimpse of sky is visible.

This painting is known in many versions, of which four stand out from the rest, although a long interval separates each of the four in point of quality. There are in addition two other versions, now apparently lost, but which may possibly be identical with two existing paintings. These six, then, will be taken in order, as they are first known to have appeared.

The first, both in time and in quality, is undoubtedly the version now in the Frick collec- *3:frontispiece* tion in New York. It is also by far the best known; it appeared in six famous exhibitions in this country between its purchase in 1866 by Henry Huth and its sale to Frick in 1912; since Frick's death in 1919 it has been regularly on display in the collection which he then bequeathed to New York City. It is generally and confidently ascribed to Holbein, but, while there are ample grounds for supposing the ascription to be correct (grounds which, as will be seen, have received further support from the X-ray photographic examination which was made of the picture in 1952), it is necessary to utter a word of caution. The history of the picture is only known for certain since 1858; there are two other blank

7

patches in its history, during the eighteenth century and between 1813 and 1858; and the first hundred years of its history are only known from a legend, which if it were not for its circumstantial detail, it would be hard to credit.

It is, however, a strong probability that the painting now in the Frick collection may safely be identified with that mentioned by Arthur Hopton in a letter from Madrid, dated 26 July 1631, to Thomas Howard, Earl of Arundel, the greatest collector of his age. In it he wrote:

The Picture of Sir Tho: More is in Rome in the Cardinall Crescentios House & is not to bee had for any price as Marques [de la Torre] tells mee.

In 1681 Baldinucci records it in the same place, and tells the following story,[1] presumably a tradition in the Crescenzi family. The picture, he says, belonged to Henry VIII and was kept by him in a room with other portraits of famous men of ancient and modern times; on the day of More's death (after the King had reproached her), Anne Boleyn cast her eyes on it and, seized with remorse on seeing the expressive face of her enemy still seeming to look at her, exclaimed 'Oh me! he still seems in this picture to be alive', opened the window and threw it into the street with her own hands; thence, although damaged, it was picked up and carried away by a passer-by, and eventually reached Rome. Now the value of this story as evidence is questionable, but some support is lent to it by an anecdote first printed by Dr Augustus Jessop.[2] Occupied with the notice of Roger North for the *Dictionary of National Biography*, Jessop found among North's papers a note concerning a portrait of Gregory XIV which North's brother Montague had purchased in Marseilles in 1693. North wrote:

This picture is judged to be by Pomerantius, painter to Gregory XIV, who was in England *tempore* Henry VIII, concerning whom the following story is told. The picture of Sir T. More done by Holbein was in Whitehall when the news was brought to Henry VIII that Sir Thomas More was beheaded. And the King fell into a passion upon the news, and running to the picture, tore it down and threw it out of the window. And the picture in the fall broke in three pieces; but Pomerantius then coming by, took it up, carried it home, and so put it together and mended the columns that it is not to be discovered that it was ever broke.

Obviously 'Gregory XIV' here is a mistake for Gregory XIII, who reigned 1572–85, and was indeed a patron of Niccolò Circigani, Il Pomarancio (1519–90). Pomarancio, on the other hand, would only have been sixteen or seventeen at the time of More's execution, and there is no evidence that he was ever in England. But much later, about 1580, he did paint a representation of the execution of More among the frescoes he did for the English College at Rome (see p. 44). Again, there are cracks in the panel on which the Frick version is

---

[1] *Notizie de' Professori del Disegno*, II, p. 319. Filippo Baldinucci (1624–96) was well considered in his day as a man of erudition, and respected as the adviser of Cardinal Leopoldo de' Medici. He was the author of several other compilations besides the *Notizie* (which may fairly be said to rank as the first critical history of art), which appeared in Florence in 1681 and were dedicated to the Grand Duke Cosimo III.

[2] *The Athenaeum*, no. 3060 (19 June 1886), p. 820.

painted, which were clearly visible until the restoration of 1952 (see fig. 3). As the careful writer of the entry in the Frick Catalogue, Mr Collins Baker, observes:

'Four vertical cracks have been mended, making a slightly dissonant patch of black on the front of the cap, and discolouring the flesh-tones across the eyebrow, nose and chin. There are small patches here and there of darker colour, where the original surface has fallen and been restored, as well as evidence of old repairs on the curtains.'[1]

This hardly agrees with North's version of the legend; moreover, there are few sixteenth-century pictures which are not cracked, through the absence or failure to work of the cradle, the woven lattice of thin strips of wood designed to prevent the wooden panel from warping and cracking. Finally, if a Holbein portrait of More ever was in the possession of Henry VIII, and it is not improbable that there was,[2] it had certainly left his possession by 1542, since there is no mention of any portrait of More in the royal inventory made in that year.

With that small piece of negative evidence in favour of the legend, we may pass to the later history of the portrait. Very probably it remained in the Crescenzi family until the latter died out during the eighteenth century. Then most likely it passed to some member of the Bonelli family, and certainly to Angelo Bonelli, who brought it to England, perhaps before 1809 and by 1811 at the latest. By that date Henry Bone had made a miniature copy of it in enamel. His squared drawing for this is in the National Portrait Gallery;[3] it bears two dates, 1809, crossed out, and 1813, and the inscription 'Mr Bonelli'. Bone may have made more than one version of his enamel copy; it must have caused considerable public interest at the time and an indifferent engraving was made of it (see p. 66). More interesting, at some time about 1900, C. Stryienski[4] saw a Bone enamel and records that it was inscribed with the date 1811, and was supposed to have been done after 'an original' at Todi, where from the sixteenth century both the Crescenzi and Bonelli families had property. This is the nearest evidence so far available that the picture which belonged to the Crescenzi and the picture which belonged to Bonelli are the same.

After 1813, there is another but probably less important gap, and the picture disappears till 1858. In that year George Scharf saw and sketched the picture at the London dealer, Farrer's. Scharf had then only just become Secretary of the National Portrait Gallery; he became its first director in 1882, and retired and was created K.C.B. in 1895. To him the Gallery owes its present honoured position, and without him the study of portraiture in this country would today be vastly poorer. In 1863,[5] Scharf noted that Farrer had told him

[1] *Catalogue of the Frick Collection* (Pittsburgh, 1949), vol. 1, pp. 96–8.

[2] If this is so, it may have been presented to the King, not long after it was painted, by More himself, rather than have been sequestrated in 1534 with More's other possessions, when it would hardly have been hung in a gallery of portraits of famous men. Van Mander (*Schilderboeck*, 1604) and Von Sandrart (*Teutsche Akademie*, 1675) both tell a story of the King's visiting More and admiring his many Holbeins; More offers the pictures to the King, who refuses them saying he would rather have the painter, and takes Holbein into his service. The story is full of improbabilities, but may contain a kernel of truth.

[3] Bone Drawings, vol. II, p. 64.

[4] *La Galérie du Régent Philippe, Duc d'Orléans*, 1913, p. 192.

[5] Sir G. Scharf, MS Notebooks in N.P.G. Archives, SSB 50, p. 58.

that he had sold the picture to a Hungarian nobleman and that it had originally been brought to England by Bonelli; in the following year Scharf was told by 'Dr Rock'[1] that this painting had been brought back to England and sold to Huth, from whom it passed in 1912, as has been said, to Frick.

When it left England, for what *The Times* described as 'a very high price'—it was supposed to be about £50,000—nobody then disputed that the English owner had the right to sell abroad this painting of one of England's greatest men. The new owner was Henry Clay Frick, former Chairman of Carnegie Brothers and the U.S. Steel Corporation. Frick had been inspired by the example of the collection formed by Sir Richard Wallace (1818–90) and bequeathed to the British nation, with an endowment, by his widow. We know it as the Wallace Collection. Similarly, on Frick's death in 1919 his collection, including the Holbein portrait of More, became the property of the city of New York, where it is magnificently maintained, open to the public, in the Frick house on Fifth Avenue, over-looking Central Park. Frick had collected one other Holbein. A competent painter and critic, Charles Ricketts, visiting the collection, described how he was 'overwhelmed by it and its situation'. 'Imagine', he wrote to Sydney Cockerell, 'Sir Thomas More, the beautiful saint, and Cromwell, the monster, united in history, art and tragedy, now facing each other, united by Holbein and time and chance.'

[1] Probably Daniel Rock (1799–1871), the Catholic ecclesiologist, who was one of the first six students who went to Rome in December 1813 on the re-opening of the English College. He returned to England in 1825 and was prominent in the 'London Mission' and in the movement to restore the Catholic hierarchy in England. In 1852 he became one of the first canons of Southwark, and in 1862 sat on the committee formed to carry out the objects of the special exhibition at the South Kensington Museum, which was later established as the Victoria and Albert Museum.

4. OTHER VERSIONS OF THE SINGLE PORTRAIT

THERE are only two other versions of the Holbein portrait with a history going back as far as that put forward for the Frick version. But both pictures disappear before the end of the eighteenth century, and cannot be identified with any of the existing versions. Even more tantalizing, there are many single references to 'Holbeins' or pictures 'on board' of More of which no further record is known. One of the earliest of these occurs in von Sandrart's crabbed, self-laudatory fragment of autobiography, written in the third person, which appears at the end of the second volume of the *Teutsche Akademie*. He visited England in the latter part of the 1620s for the specific purpose, he says, of measuring the best and most beautiful works of art in England, carefully copying them and enriching his book of studies therewith. Among the many he treated thus in the long garden gallery of Thomas Howard, Earl of Arundel, were Holbein's famous pair of pictures executed as wall-decorations for the Hanseatic merchants of the Steelyard, the Triumphs of Riches and Poverty, and the even more celebrated More family group (see pp. 18ff.), and other notable examples of the 'foolish curiosity in enquiringe for the pieces of Holbein' to which the Earl confessed in a letter to Sir Dudley Carlton in 1619.[1] Among them was a picture of 'Thomae Mori Gross canzlers des königs Heinrich des achte'. Von Sandrart makes it quite clear that it was by Holbein; he can hardly have confused it with the family group, which he described in detail elsewhere; the precision of the title precludes the possibility that he could have mistaken it for the *figliolo de Tomase More*, which appears in the 1655 inventory. And yet, in the same inventory, there is no mention of a Holbein of Thomas More. Sandrart left England soon after in alarm at the assassination of the Duke of Buckingham, and at some time in the ensuing twenty-seven years, Lord Arundel must have parted with his More, which then disappears completely.[2]

Again, in 1725 George Vertue the engraver and antiquary (1684–1756), whose exhaustive notebooks provide the raw material for so much of the early history of the arts in this country, noted another at Barnborough Hall near Barnsley in Yorkshire. Barnborough was the seat of the Cresacre More branch of More's descendants; they possessed a number of relics of their ancestor, among them 'Sir Thomas More painted on bord an Antient picture —half lenght by Holbein a piece always preserved in the family.'[3] The surviving relics have passed by descent and marriage to the Eyston family of East Hendred, but the only

---

[1] Quoted in M.F.S. Harvey, *The Life, Correspondence, and Collections of Thomas Howard, Earl of Arundel*, 1921, p. 162.

[2] Cf. *Lebenslauf und Kunstwerke des . . . Herrn Joachims von Sandrart*, Nürnberg, 1675, pp. 5–6.

[3] Vertue, *Notebooks*, II, p. 75. Here, and from now on, all references to Vertue's *Notebooks* will be cited by the volume and page numbers of the Walpole Society's edition.

28 single portrait of More there now is a later copy on canvas. Vertue records other versions in less detail, some of which, those 'on board', may well have been of some antiquity.[1]

From early on, versions also existed on the continent of Europe. Denucé's admirable compilation records several portraits of More mentioned in inventories at Antwerp between 1621 and 1681,[2] quite apart from Queen Christina of Sweden's version and the Rubens copy, which will be described later (see p. 62). Lastly, during the latter part of the eighteenth century, a critical period in the history of all these versions of the Holbein portrait, a number of portraits supposedly of More passed through the London sale rooms, any of which could be one of the paintings known to have appeared or disappeared at that time.

THE ORLEANS VERSION

The portrait in the Frick Collection, then, has a history which appears to go back to Hopton's letter to Arundel in 1631. Attached to it also is a legend which not impossibly carries the provenance back to the source. There are two other versions, early attributed to Holbein, which are not certainly identifiable with any painting known to exist now. First, if only because it has frequently been confused with the Frick portrait, there is 4 that which we may, since it was the Regent of France who owned it longest, term the Orleans version. It is first recorded in the possession of an equally distinguished patron of the arts, Queen Christina of Sweden. In May 1656, the year after her reception into the Church, there is listed in an inventory of goods in the house of Don Ferdinando de Yllan, her resident in Antwerp, and destined to be sent to Rome, *le poortraict de Holbain, de Thomas Morus*.[3] In 1668 Christina settled permanently in Rome, where she filled the Palazzo Riaro with her vast collection of manuscripts, books and paintings. There in 1689 she died. Her manuscripts went to the Vatican library, to which, even in that magnificent collection, it constituted a notable accession; but her pictures and other works of art were dispersed owing to an unforeseen circumstance. The daughter of Gustavus Adolphus died on 19 April, making as the principal heir to her art collection her favourite cardinal, Decio Azzolino. He died at the beginning of the following July and his heir, Pompeo Azzolino, held a great sale which lost to Rome the most part of the great collection —with the portrait of More it contained. It was this sale, coming so soon after Baldinucci's description of the portrait then in the possession of the Crescenzi family, which has induced the supposition that Christina acquired her portrait of More from this source, and that it was the painting which later belonged to the Duke of Orleans which is now in the Frick Collection.

The collection passed to the Duke of Bracciano, who in turn died in 1713, and then after tortuous negotiations it was bought by Philippe, Duke of Orleans and Regent of France, in 1721. In the same year the pictures were brought to Paris and there they remained until the end of the century. The portrait of More is recorded as being on exhibition in the Palais Royal in 1727, and in the Orleans inventories of 1752 and 1785. When the Orleans collec-

[1] See the catalogue below, 30, 34 and 35.
[2] J. Denucé, *The Antwerp Art Galleries in the Seventeenth Century*, 1932, pp. 30, 167, 238 and 304.
[3] J. Denucé, *The Antwerp Art Galleries*, p. 178.

tions were dispersed after the French Revolution, the larger part was sold in London, including the portrait of More. In 1793 it came up as lot 11 in the sale held by Wilson of Pall Mall in April of that year,[1] and thereafter it disappears. There is a possibility—no more —that it is one of the two portraits of More which first appear about this time, but before we consider this, note must be taken of the other version early recorded and now lost.

THE LUMLEY VERSION

In 1590 an inventory was made of the notable collection of John, Lord Lumley;[2] it includes a picture described as *Sir Thomas Moore, Lo: Chauncellor, drawne by Haunce Holbyn*. It is   5 possible that Lord Lumley inherited the picture from his father-in-law Henry FitzAlan, Earl of Arundel, who died in 1580. It is, however, unlikely that it was among the number of pictures which, when Lord Lumley died in 1609 without direct issue, passed to the great collector Thomas Howard, Earl of Arundel, the great-grandson on the female side of Henry FitzAlan. More probably it remained at Lumley, because portraits of More reputed to be by Holbein were twice sold by the Lumley family two hundred years later. The first of these, which appears as lot 15 of Christie's sale of 11 August 1785, was described as *Stated to be by Holbein*, and was bought according to a priced catalogue by 'Mr Hay of Savile Row' for £5 15s. 6d. It is possible, however, that it was bought in, because at another Lumley sale, Dawson's of 18 December 1807, another *Sir Thomas Moore, Lord Chancellor* (are the title and the spelling of the name perhaps significant?) was sold. Thereafter it too disappears.[3] It may be remarked that a number of the portraits listed in the 1590 inventory were said to be by Holbein, and Mr David Piper has shown that some at least of these were originals by him.[4]

THE LOTHIAN AND BEDFORD VERSIONS

We come now to the versions of the Holbein portrait which still exist. The earliest recorded of these is the painting now in the collection of the Marquess of Lothian, which is first noted   6:4 in a Lothian inventory of 1798. It was exhibited at the British Institution exhibition in 1864. This is an early copy of some quality, which may well be sixteenth-century work. It follows the detail of the Frick portrait very accurately, but there is a certain stiffness about the face and hands.

The Bedford version is of better quality. This, now in a private collection in Munich, is   7:5 certainly identifiable as lot 83 in Christie's sale of 30 June 1827. The seller's name was not recorded in the sale catalogue, but it has been established that it was the fifth Duke of Bedford. The picture was bought by a firm of London dealers, Nieuwenhuys, who had a branch in Brussels; they in turn sold it to the king of Holland. It appeared again in

[1] J. Stryienski, *La Galérie du Régent Philippe, Duc d'Orléans*, p. 192.
[2] Published by the Walpole Society, vol. VI (1918), p. 27.
[3] See Walpole Society, vol. VI, pp. 24–44 *passim*.
[4] *Burlington Magazine*, vol. XCIX (1957), pp. 224–231.

William II's sale at Paris in 1850 but seems to have been bought in and to have passed by descent to the collection of Prince zu Wied, where it remained until recently. A paper label inscribed with the Duke of Bedford's name and the King of Holland's seal are still affixed to the back of the panel.

This painting has been itself overlooked, and, by a curious confusion, identified with the Frick portrait. None of the most recent works on Holbein record it at all: they only refer to the Frick version. Yet two of the most distinguished, Dr Ganz's *The Paintings of Hans Holbein* and H. A. Schmid's *Hans Holbein der Jüngere*, reproduce photographs of this, the Bedford version, *as* the Frick portrait. This is all the more curious, since it contains a number of variations from the Frick image, where less good copies, such as the Lothian version, follow the Frick portrait more closely. Among these variations may be noted the absence of the projecting curl on the left cheek, the relatively even curve of the left eyebrow (where the Frick portrait has a break in the upper line), and the less protruding line of the facial bone above the right eyebrow; in fact, as will be seen, the differences follow what is generally known as the first of the two drawings known to be by Holbein.

Another variation is the introduction of a false shadow cast by the end of the curtain cord (present also in the Lothian version), on the assumption that the background was a wall, not sky. Yet the quality of the picture is such that it is difficult to believe that it is not a direct copy of the Frick version, or of an equally good lost original. Since it is painted on a thick lime-wood panel, there is some reason to suppose that the Bedford version may have been painted on the Continent rather than in England, where a thin bevelled oak panel was usual; some confirmation of this might be obtained if it were possible to establish the early history of the Frick version with more certainty. Another early version, once in the collection of Richard Tayloors and sold at Sotheby's on 27 April 1960, lot 92, appears though considerably damaged, to conform more closely to the Bedford than the Frick version.

It is tempting to try and connect the pedigrees of the four versions which together have a continuous history going back to the seventeenth century, and to equate the Orleans version which disappears in 1793 and the Lumley version which disappears between 1785 and 1807 with the Lothian version which appears in 1798 and the Bedford version which appears in 1827. But it should be remembered that the history of the Frick version is not established beyond doubt between 1681 and 1858. All that can be safely said is that three portraits of More said to be by Holbein are known to have existed before 1780; that all three disappear within the next fifty years; and that any one of three which emerge after 1830 could be any one of the three which existed before 1780—or a different picture altogether.

It should be emphasized, too, that the versions described above represent only a fraction of the total number of oil paintings of More which still exist, and there must be many more which have eluded the catalogue at the end of this book. One of these may yet provide the crucial link to connect the few known facts about the early history of these versions into a more satisfactory series of provenances. At present, the most remarkable features of those that survive are, first, their quantity and, secondly, their close adherance to the original

Holbein likeness. The persistence of demand for portraits of More is a tribute to the enduring fame of the subject; the repetition—so far as the competence of later painters allowed it—of Holbein's portrait is a tribute to the artist. What variation is observable is due, in the main, to the influence of other sources, in particular the engravings uninhibited by any debt to Holbein; and to special circumstances, as, for example, the desire to depict More as martyr rather than chancellor. A good example of this latter influence is to be seen in the best and earliest of three portraits at Knole. Here a cross has been substituted for the rose hanging from the chain of SS, and an open book for the scroll in order to introduce a legend which, although damaged, must refer to the cause for which More died.

The list in Appendix A, then, can give some notion of the popularity of the Holbein oil painting of More, and the frequency with which it was copied. It may also shew, to some extent, how the original image deteriorated and changed with the passage of time. How far and where it is safe to detect the hand of Holbein himself are questions which must be postponed to a later chapter.

Postscript. Evidence has since come to light which shews that the Lumley version was, in fact, sold in 1785. According to a copy of the sale catalogue with contemporary annotations, 'Mr Hay thinks this to be as genuine a Holbein as any in the Kingdom'; from which it may be inferred that Mr Hay had bought the picture. A transcript by Mary Hervey of the catalogue, which in 1916 belonged to Dr Hardcastle of Newcastle upon Tyne, is in the National Portrait Gallery. According to local tradition, the portrait still at Lumley was painted to replace the picture sold in 1785. It may be noted that a More by Holbein appears in the Lumley inventory of 1772.

It may also be germane to note here a portrait listed in the inventory (now British Museum Add. MS. 38652) of the possessions of Cardinal Philip Howard, made after his death in Rome and dated 28 June 1694. On f26r appears

214. Un altro quadro di tre P[al]mi del ritratto di Tomasso Moro con cornice Liscia dorada. 6 . 0 [scudi]

The dimensions seem to indicate a picture of the size of the Frick version.

Finally, an interesting confirmation of the presence of the Orleans version in the Palais Royal is to be found in the manuscript notes of the Cambridge antiquary William Cole (now B.M. Add. MS. 5808, at folio 130 V.).

I saw in Nov 1766 an indifferent picture of Bp Fisher, with one of Sir Tho. More, Abp Plunket &c on a staircase near the Prior's Apartment of the English Benedictines at Paris; but a most admirable one of Sir Tho. More, by Holbein, in the fine collection of the Duke of Orleans at the Palais Royal at Paris also.[1]

[1] I owe the first reference to Mr Piper, and the last two to Dr Herbruggen.

5. THE DRAWINGS AT WINDSOR

No such doubts hang over the authenticity of the history of the two drawings of More which Holbein executed. Both form part of the large collection of Holbein studies, once bound up in a book, which have been, apart from some brief intervals, in royal possession since the mid-sixteenth century, and have been attributed to Holbein since that time. They are now at Windsor. The only doubt—since a number of the drawings have been subjected to reworking—is how much represents Holbein's original work.

1:1   The first (Windsor 12225) is the slighter of the two; the outline is in black chalk, with red for the lips and details of the eyes and lightly applied to give the complexion; the contours have largely been reworked and the brown wash on the cap is also later in date. The principal authority on the Windsor drawings writes of it 'the general effect is empty';[1] and it is difficult to say how much of the original work survives. Nevertheless it is clearly allied to the Holbein image, and of the two corresponds most closely perhaps to the Basel pen and ink sketch of the family group.

2:2   The second drawing (Windsor 12268), however, is by far the better portrait. Executed in black, brown, red and yellow chalks, it is worked out in much greater detail and exhibits a far greater degree of penetration. It differs from the first in the drawing of the cap, which is firmer, and of the hair, which curls in from the left temple instead of being swept back; a double line indicates the position of the chain of SS. An interesting point, and one to which we shall return, is that there is a disparity in the angle of vision from which the right and left sides of the face are seen which gives the impression the right eye is incorrectly sited; it is seen more fully than the angle of the head will permit, an inconsistency caused, perhaps, by a movement of the sitter while Holbein was drawing.[2] This drawing is also pricked along the outlines (a method of transfer) and so was almost certainly used in the early stages of a subsequent painting. This has encouraged the surmise that it was in fact the sketch of More's head for one of Holbein's finished paintings. This surmise has been further supported by the existence of six other studies also at Windsor for the other members of More's household; Holbein may have made others of the remaining figures which have not survived.

The history of the drawings has been established not perhaps completely, but more nearly so than any of the other Holbein originals.[3] The first years after Holbein's death (as sketches, he most likely kept them until then) are obscure, but at some point after 1547 they

[1] K. T. Parker, *The Drawings of Hans Holbein . . . at Windsor Castle*, 1945, p. 36.

[2] It may also be further evidence of Holbein's use of a tracing apparatus for sketching outlines (Parker, p. 30).

[3] The account in K. T. Parker, op. cit., supersedes those of all previous authorities.

were in the possession of Edward VI. Some time after the king's death, the book in which the drawings were contained passed into the possession of Henry FitzAlan, Earl of Arundel, where it must have found a place among the treasures which that earliest of Holbein collectors amassed at Nonsuch.[1] On his death in 1580, it was inherited by John, Lord Lumley, and was duly noted in the inventory of 1590 (see p. 13) as 'A greate booke of Pictures doone by Haunce Holbyn of certayne Lordes, Ladyes, gentlemen and gentlewomen of King Henry the 8: his tyme, their names subscribed by Sr. John Cheke secretary to King Edward the 6 wch book was King Edward the 6 [th's]'. This provenance may be considered entirely reliable, although the 'names subscribed by Sr. John Cheke' have now been lost and the present inscriptions are in later hands, whose identifications are not always correct.

After Lumley's death in 1609, there is a brief period of uncertainty, which ends with the exchange described by Van der Doort in his catalogue of Charles I's collection in 1636. To obtain the Raphael of *St. George* (now in the National Gallery at Washington), Charles I gave Lord Pembroke 'the book of Holbein's drawings; wherein are many heads, which were done with Crayons'. Lord Pembroke then immediately gave the book to Thomas Howard, Earl of Arundel. That it should have been in royal possession about 1630, the probable time of this exchange, suggests that in 1609 it passed with a number of Lumley's other books to the talented Prince Henry, on whose premature death it would have gone to his brother Charles. Arundel found it convenient to live abroad after 1642. He kept his possessions with him including, possibly but not certainly, the 'great booke', until he died at Padua in 1646. Family disputes then broke up the Arundel collections, only some of which returned to England. In 1675, however, the book is mentioned, as having returned to the royal collection, in Alexander Browne's *Appendix of the Art of Painting* (the last of several derivatives of Norgate's *Miniatura* which provide some confirmation of the book's movements between 1630 and 1675). From the time of the last Stuart king the drawings were forgotten until Caroline of Ansbach, George II's consort, discovered them at the back of a desk in Kensington Palace, two hundred years after the artist had worked on them. The English royal family has since retained these 'heads'; and with them the sketches of the More household that Holbein drew probably by way of preparation for the painting of the family group. Queen Caroline, it seems, personally discovered their existence and revived their prestige by decorating her apartment at Richmond with them. The extension of their fame in terms of engraving will be referred to later.

The relation of the two drawings to each other and to the other Holbein likenesses will be considered shortly; in the meantime, it is to be borne in mind in this connection that they are the only representations of the man, chancellor and humanist that may be said with absolute confidence to have come indisputably and demonstrably from the hand of Holbein. If, then, England has lost the portrait of More which appears most likely to be that which Holbein completed in 1527, she retains the drawing which may be—as the inaccuracy mentioned above suggests—Holbein's first sketch from the life.

[1] It seems possible that the drawings, if not already in a book, were bound up or rebound during the reign of Edward VI; see Parker, p. 8.

6. THE HOLBEIN FAMILY GROUP PORTRAIT

THE great painting of the More family group, executed about the same time as the single portrait, is lost. It was, perhaps, not only the most vivid of Holbein's likenesses of More, but a work of cardinal importance in the development of portraiture: it has been described as the 'first example of an intimate group portrait not of devotional or ceremonial character to be painted this side of the Alps'. Such is the magnitude of the artistic loss sustained by the total disappearance of this work, a loss the greater since we do not know what inspired More to suggest or Holbein to adopt this revolutionary method of portraiture.

401 There were ten—or possibly eleven—figures depicted. In the middle was More himself, shown full length and seated, looking to the right, very much in the attitude of the single portrait, but with an expression more open and less guarded than in the formal portrait. His father, Sir John More, sat on his right, and Anne Cresacre, who married More's son John was between and behind them. On the extreme left of the picture were More's daughter Elizabeth Dauncey and Margaret Giggs, the fellow student and *sœur de lait* of More's daughter, who married Dr John Clement, also long a member of More's household. On More's left were his daughters Cecily Heron and Margaret Roper, and his second wife Alice, with her tame monkey by her side; behind them were John More and More's fool Henry Patenson. The wall of the room in which the group is sitting formed the background. On the left was a sideboard with a canopy on which were a bottle, some cups, a salver and a vase of flowers; in the middle was a clock with hanging weights; to the right was a doorway leading to another room (in the best of the later copies, the Nostell version, John Harris, More's faithful secretary, is shewn in this doorway—the possible eleventh figure—but he does not appear in Holbein's own pen and ink drawing now at Basel); on the extreme right was a window with a jug, salver and books on the sill. Some books and a low stool lay on the floor in the foreground.[1] The picture was executed in 'distemper [watercolour, or perhaps tempera] on cloth' according to van Mander. In this it resembled the two famous allegorical paintings, the Triumphs of Riches and Poverty, executed about 1532 or 1533 for the merchants of the steelyard, with which, as will be seen, it was probably destroyed.

[1] These details are those shewn in the Basel sketch. The Nostell version differs: there are two vases of flowers on the sideboard and also some musical instruments (these last may well have been in the lost original, because there is in the drawing a viol roughly indicated next to the clock with a note, probably in Holbein's hand, that the instruments were on a shelf); the foreground is clear of books, and there is a dog at More's feet; Elizabeth Dauncey and Margaret Giggs have exchanged positions; finally, Alice More is shewn sitting instead of kneeling (a change also indicated by a 'Holbein' note on the Basel sketch).

The history of so important a painting has naturally been the subject of much discussion and controversy, but the existence of a number of copies from an early date has caused no little confusion, only recently resolved by the learned Dr Kurz. The original must date from 1527: the sitters' ages, inscribed both on the Basel sketch and on the copies, establish that the picture must have been finished before More's fifty-first birthday on 7 February 1528.[1] Such an intimate portrait must surely have been intended for More's own possession. After his death it may have been sequestrated or it may have passed to his descendants; probably the former, since it is next heard of in the possession of the collector Andreas de Loo, who died in 1590.

De Loo had been in England since at least 1570, and was one of Lord Burghley's many agents in the Low Countries, where he probably combined business interests with the gathering of political intelligence. He was employed in the peace negotiations of 1587–8, and must have died before 30 August 1590, when his papers are recorded as having been sent to the Queen for her perusal, after his death.[2] That the More family group was in his possession is a fact we owe to the biography of Holbein in Carel van Mander's *Schilder-boeck*, an invaluable if not always accurate collection of notes on the North European painters up to his time, first published in 1604, shortly before the author's death. Van Mander further records that at the time of writing, after de Loo's death, the Holbein original had passed 'to a nobleman, the nephew of Thomas More, also named More', who had bought it from his estate. This nephew of More cannot be identified: the most likely candidate is perhaps More's grandson, Thomas More (1531–1606), the head of the Barnborough branch of the family. But as a staunch recusant, who had only just emerged from a long imprisonment in the Marshalsey (1582–1586), he is unlikely to have been in a position to purchase so famous a picture. Vertue,[3] who had read van Mander, identified him with William Roper and the picture consequently with the Nostell version, now in the collection of Lord St Oswald. However, as Dr Kurz points out, Roper died in 1578, twelve years before de Loo; further, van Mander describes the picture as in watercolours, whereas the Nostell version is in oil; finally, the name of the buyer is expressly stated to have been More. Only one other detail of this transaction may be noted: elsewhere,[4] Vertue notes that the person who bought the picture on de Loo's death was 'Mr Cope'. The editors of the Walpole Society's transcript of the Notebooks tentatively identify him with Sir Walter Cope,[5] who died in 1614, and it seems likely that Vertue's note is the result of a misreading of van Mander's rambling account, in which he is describing this picture together with three other pictures, which he records as having passed from de Loo to 'Mr Coop'.

[1] It may, however, have been completed earlier: see below, p. 26.

[2] *Calendar of Domestic State Papers 1547–80*, pp. 400–1, 697; *Calendar 1581–90*, pp. 424, 427, 505, 658, 686–7; *Calendar of Venetian State Papers 1581–91*, nos. 441, 526.

[3] *Notebooks*, IV, 11ff.   [4] *Notebooks*, I, 154.

[5] Vertue describes him elsewhere as a 'curious collector of pictures'; he built Holland House, where there were a number of old pictures in Vertue's time, one of which, Holbein's portrait of More's friend the astronomer Nicolas Kratzer, had certainly belonged to de Loo. Cope's only daughter and heiress, Isabel, married Henry Rich, 1st Earl of Holland and great-grandson of Sir Richard Rich whose perjury served to convict More.

A little later the picture passed to Thomas Howard, Earl of Arundel, and it was listed in the inventory made in 1655 after the death of Lady Arundel with the two other great Holbeins painted in the same way, *The Triumph of Riches* and *The Triumph of Poverty*, which Arundel had acquired from the Royal collection. With a large number of his other pictures, the More family group was bought by the brothers Franz and Bernhard von Imstenrädt, and it is described in some detail in the verse catalogue *Iconophylacium sive Artis Apelleae Thesaurarium* which they produced in 1667. By then, it is interesting to note, the condition of the picture had deteriorated; the *Iconophylacium* laments that it was painted in watercolours, and an earlier catalogue of their collection describes it firmly as *alquanto rovinato*, 'somewhat damaged'. The object of both these catalogues was to sell the brothers' collection, and in this they finally succeeded in 1670, when it passed to Carl von Liechtenstein, Bishop of Olmütz. By him the pictures were divided, part going to the episcopal palace at Olmütz and part to his summer seat at Kremsier. But now only fifteen pictures from the Imstenrädt collection are to be seen at Kremsier, and it seems all too probable that the More family group, with the two *Triumphs*, was destroyed in a fire which gutted part of the building in 1752.[1] One last curious circumstance may be noted. In April 1727 the College of the Society of Jesus at Olmütz put on a play in honour of their then bishop, Wilhelm Adalbert Liebsteinski. The play was called *Heroica in Adversis Constantia Thomae Mori* and it displayed in dramatic form the life and martyrdom of Thomas More. Several of the *dramatis personae*[2] were to be found depicted in Holbein's group, and it is not unthinkable that the play may be the last sign of the existence of the picture.

THE DRAWING OF THE FAMILY GROUP

402:8   The Basel sketch is executed in pen and ink on paper. It is not like a preliminary study: on the other hand, it differs from the Nostell version in several important particulars. In two of these, it will be remembered, the changes are indicated in a hand generally supposed to be that of Holbein. These changes seem to indicate that the drawing is a record of the painting, made before it was finished. It is possible to surmise that some of them may have been authorized in discussion with More. Certainly, Elizabeth Dauncey, as More's own daughter, is more suitably placed nearer to her father than Margaret Giggs, his ward, although the absence of the leaning figure detracts from the unity of the group. More might have liked Holbein to include his clerk, as well as his jester. So, also, it might have been by his wish that the pet dog was brought in at his feet, as a counterpart to Dame Alice's monkey. The names and ages of the sitters are inscribed on the drawing in a second hand, which was for long supposed to be that of More himself. Dr Pächt, however, has demonstrated that it is more likely that of Nicolas Kratzer, who taught astronomy to More's daughter and was a

---

[1] The evidence is set out at greater length in Dr Kurz's conclusive article in the *Burlington Magazine*, LXXXIII (1943), pp. 279ff.

[2] There is also a generalized character, Blepander, who bears a curious resemblance to the 'Common Man' of Mr Bolt's play.

Figure 5. The Bedford version (7)

Figure 6. A typical variant: the earliest Knole version (19)

Io. Clemens.   Hythlodæus.   Tho. Morus. Pet. Aegid.

Figure 7. The group in the garden. Woodcut, probably by Ambrosius Holbein, in *Utopia*, Basel, 1518 (701)

FAMILIA THOMÆ MORI ANGL: CANCELL:

Thomas Morus Aᵗ 50. Alicia Thomæ Mori uxor Aᵗ 57. Iohannes Morus pater Aᵗ 76. Iohannes Morus Thomæ filius Aᵗ 19. Anna Grisacria Iohannis Mori Sponsa Aᵗ 15. Margareta Ropera Thomæ Mori filia Aᵗ 22.
Elisabeta Damea Thomæ Mori filia Aᵗ 21. Cæcilia Heroina Thomæ Mori filia Aᵗ 20. Margareta Giga Clementis uxor Mori filiabus Condiscipula et cognata Aᵗ 22. Henricus Patensonus Thomæ Mori morio Aᵗ 40.

Figure 8. The Basel Sketch of the Family Group (402)

Figure 9. The Nostell version of the Family Group (403)

Figure 10. The National Portrait Gallery version of the Family Group (404)

constant visitor at his house.[1] The date '1530' has been added later by a third hand, probably in the seventeenth or eighteenth century.

The drawing may have been made at Erasmus's request, and it seems likely that Holbein took it himself when he returned to Switzerland in August 1528 to deliver to More's old friend. For some unexplained reason Erasmus did not acknowledge the gift until the following year, but his gratitude was, as always, vividly expressed in letters to More and Margaret Roper.[2] His opinion of the likeness, 'so well has Holbein depicted the whole family for me that if I had been with you I could not have seen more' is an admirable testimony of the success of Holbein's portraiture. When Erasmus died, the drawing passed to his great friend Bonifacius Amerbach, the youngest son of the great printer. It remained in the Amerbach family until 1662, when it was sold with the rest of the collection made by Bonifacius and his son Basilius to the city of Basel where, in the Kupferstichkabinett, it still remains.

Perhaps the most important unresolved question, however, does not concern these or later versions; it is the novelty, and the origin and purpose, of the family group as a composition. Erasmus does not remark on it, but, since the arts were less self-conscious then than now, it is not to be expected that he should. That he only praises Holbein's executive skill and gives him no credit for the idea may encourage the supposition that More first thought of a group portrait. More's household was an unusual—unique—institution: its corporate unity may well have suggested to him that a portrait of himself alone was not complete without the others. Again, Erasmus had asked him to find employment for Holbein: where was it more easily to hand than in his own family?

If it is possible that the immediate idea was More's, the execution was all Holbein's, and where did he find his model? Mr Piper has recently pointed out that there is an absence of focus which cannot be explained by the alterations for which More may have been responsible. But if, he suggests, there is an echo here of the family group in the Palazzo Ducale at Mantua by Mantegna (whose influence has been remarked elsewhere in Holbein's work), the composition may also be an example of the kind of adaptation of a religious formula to a secular purpose, which was no doubt thrust on Holbein from his earliest years by the changing sense of values in the city in which he grew up. In the 'Darmstadt Madonna', which he painted in 1526, the Meyer family are grouped round, and radiate from, the Madonna and Child in the top centre: if there were a similar nucleus in the empty foreground of the More family group, it would become an Adoration.[3]

[1] O. Pächt, *Burlington Magazine*, LXXXIV (1944), pp. 138ff.

[2] Erasmus: *Epistolae*, ed. Allen, 2211 and 2212 (3 September and 6 September 1529).

[3] See David Piper, 'Hans Holbein the Younger in England' (the Fred Cook Memorial Lecture, 1 May 1963), published in the *Journal of the Royal Society of Arts*, vol. CXI (1963), pp. 736-55.

7. ROWLAND LOCKY AND THE LATER FAMILY GROUP PORTRAITS

IT is tempting to suppose that the three copies of Holbein's group, all attributed with varying degrees of certainty to Rowland Locky, were made when, according to van Mander, the original returned to the family after the death of Andreas de Loo. Against this may be set the puzzling fact that the family must, in this case, have parted with the original again very shortly after they recovered it, and—a slighter objection—Vertue's unsupported statement that the picture was bought not by the family but by Cope. There can be little doubt, as the alterations indicated on the Basel drawing shew, that it was the original from which Locky made his copies, whether or not the original belonged at the time to the family. It is possible that the number of copies made was necessitated by the fact that the original did not then belong to them, but on the whole the first hypothesis seems the most likely.

Not much is known of Rowland Locky. All the details of his life, so far discovered, will be found in Miss Auerbach's exhaustive life of Nicholas Hilliard.[1] Locky was apprenticed to Hilliard in 1581; he is mentioned among the first painters of England by Francis Meres in *Palladis Tamia* (London, 1598). He died in 1616. The best of his copies is the Nostell version, which must be a pretty faithful version of Holbein. Indeed, it was long assumed to be at any rate partly the work of Holbein. This theory was based on a misreading of the signature as '*Richardus Locky Fec. ano.* 1530'; Holbein, it was concluded, had made a copy of his original three years later (the ages inscribed on the copy are the same as those on the original), which had either been left unfinished or had been damaged, and was completed by Locky, who added his own name while retaining the original date. Dr Kurz has, however, recently pointed out that the inscription is defective at beginning and end; 'Richardus' might well be 'Rowlandus', which would remove an awkward discrepancy, and the date is almost completely effaced.[2] It would, therefore, be much more plausible to suppose that it was painted at much the same time as the second version, now in the National Portrait Gallery, which is clearly inscribed 1593. If this is so, it would be safe to suppose that the picture had been painted for William Roper's son who succeeded him as protonotary of the King's Bench, for it came by descent to Nostell Priory from the Ropers' house, Well Hall, at Eltham, when Susanna Henshaw, the ultimate heiress, married Sir Rowland Winn of Nostell. It was still at Well Hall when Vertue first saw it, when Thomas Rawlinson the book-collector saw it and described it at length for Thomas Hearne, who

---

[1] Erna Auerbach: *Nicholas Hilliard*, London, 1962. [2] *Burlington Magazine*, XCIX (1957), pp. 13–16. The original reading of the date may have been suggested by the erroneous date on the Basel sketch.

incorporated the description in his edition of Roper's life of More, and later when the Reverend John Lewis saw it in March 1716.[1]

The version in the National Portrait Gallery differs considerably from the Nostell version. The left hand part is copied from Holbein's group, but Alice More and Margaret Giggs are omitted, and also Henry Patenson, whose place is filled by the figure of Elizabeth Dauncey, transposed from her original position. On the right hand side is the head of the senior branch of the family in 1593, More's grandson Thomas (d. 1606) with his wife and two sons. All the detail of the background on the right has gone, and across the full width of the picture are a series of seven coats of arms, the first of which carries the significant motto CHRISTIANO CATHOLICO MORE. It was this picture, without doubt, that was seen by William Burton (1575–1645) in Locky's studio, and described as 'a neat piece in oil, containing in one table the picture of Sir John More, a judge of the King's Bench, *temp.* Henry VIII, and of his wife, and of Sir Thomas More, lord chancellor, his son and wife, and of all the lineal heirs male descended from them, together with each man's wife unto that present year'[2]— an inaccurate but unmistakeable description. Vertue was given a circumstantial account of its subsequent history by the Mores of Barnborough, whom he visited in 1728.[3] The picture passed to Cresacre More (1592–1649) who appears in it as a young man. From him it was borrowed by William Lenthall (1591–1662), Speaker of the House of Commons, who was connected with the family and wanted a copy made; then the civil war broke out, ' & Lenthal being a great Man in those times still retain'd the picture & at lenght possitively refus'd to return it'. The Mores were forced to sell their estate at Gobions and moved to Yorkshire. Cresacre More's son threatened legal action to recover the picture, but without success; it was still at the Lenthalls' house at Besselsleigh when John Aubrey saw it in the time of the Speaker's son Sir John Lenthall (1625–81).[4] Vertue saw it there again in 1721, but when he saw it next in 1727 (and again in 1741) it had been moved to their other house at Burford, which they had bought from Lord Falkland.[5] It was sold out of the family in 1833 and passed through several hands; eventually it came into the possession of Mr E. J. Horniman, who also owned the Lenthalls' seat at Burford Priory. He bequeathed the picture to the nation whenever the Priory should again be sold; and so it reached London in 1935.

The last copy of Holbein's group which has been attributed to Locky is a miniature. It is closely related to the picture in the National Portrait Gallery, but differs notably in two respects. In the first place, there is, where in the Nostell version a doorway leading to another room is shown, a vista of a formal garden, with a distant prospect of London, depicted with an attention to the beauties of nature unusual at the time except in the work of Nicholas

405

[1] *Vita D. Thomae Mori*, ed. Hearne, Oxford 1716, pp. XII–XVII, and *The Life and Death of Sir Thomas More*, ed. Lewis, London 1729, pp. 168–71. Details of the picture's subsequent history, and of the minor changes effected on the several occasions on which it has been cleaned (first by Thornhill in 1715), will be found in M. W. Brockwell, *Catalogue of the Pictures at Nostell Abbey*, London 1913, pp. 75ff.

[2] J. Nichols, *History and Antiquities of the County of Leicester*, vol. III, pt. I (1800), p. 490.

[3] *Notebooks*, II, 53.

[4] *Brief Lives*, ed. Powell (London, 1949), p. 316.

[5] In his description he notes the gold lettering at the top, which is now missing, but does appear in the miniature.

Hilliard; secondly, the figure of Henry Patenson re-appears in the middle background, pulling back a curtain. It is painted in watercolours on vellum. Its history is comparatively uneventful, for it remained in the possession of the Sotheby family of Ecton Hall from the beginning of the eighteenth century until 1955, when it was sold to a private collector.[1] It is first certainly recorded in a notebook of the original purchaser, James Sotheby, in 1705 as bought from 'Lady Gerrard' (who is, as yet, unidentified) for £10 15s. It was then attributed to Holbein; but Walpole later gave it to Peter Oliver, an ascription which was still current at the time of the Tudor Exhibition in 1890. Nothing was then known of Locky's gifts and reputation as a miniaturist, but Dr Kurz has recently shown[2] that he was if anything better known as a 'limner', a fact which Miss Auerbach's discovery of his association with Hilliard has served to confirm. Both these authorities consider our miniature to be Locky's work, and it is to be observed that Vertue came to the same conclusion. In 1742 he noted

another curious limning being the family peece of Sr Thomas More and his Father son and 3 daughters. his sons wife. Cressacre—his grandson Thomas More. & his lady Scroope & their two sons. standing—a prospect of his Gardens at Chelsea appears part of his Gallery & chappel at the distance London spires very small. above this is the names of each person writ in small, —

the father of Mr Southbys. (owner) bought this limning many years ago of a Gentlewoman who was under some necessity—and was as I have heard before sold to him by a daughter of the Mores family—this picture in small is like the large one at Burford . . . (only the background is different) . . . I think this limning was done at the expense of Mr.—Thomas More after the large one (1593) . . . Qu who limned it. I guess the painter who painted the large one in oil.[3]

406   There are three other copies or variants of the family group, mostly following the Nostell version. The best of these is that now in the Eyston family collection at East Hendred, which has passed by descent and marriage direct from the Mores of Barnborough, where Vertue saw it. It has been cut down on the right side by at least a foot, and Lady More's portrait has gone, perhaps for separate exhibition, perhaps because that part of the picture was damaged. In all probability this copy dates from the seventeenth century, and it is possible to conjecture that it may have been made to replace the picture 'borrowed' by Lenthall from the only other original by Locky in the More family, then belonging to the Ropers at Well Hall.

408   Another seventeenth-century copy, now belonging to Mr W. H. M. Vane of Hutton in the Forest, consists only of the central part of the picture, the portraits of More and his father, with a single coat of arms above their heads. Lastly, there is a full-size copy, recently
407 purchased from Lord Petre of Ingatestone by the Chelsea Society and given to Crosby Hall as a memorial of the Society's founder. It is first recorded by Vertue c. 1730 as

---

[1] Sotheby's, 11 October (reproduced in catalogue).   [2] *Burlington Magazine*, XCIX (1957), pp. 13–16.
[3] *Notebooks*, V, 10–11. This account of the provenance does not wholly agree with an earlier reference where he says that the picture was offered to a daughter of Cresacre More, 'but, she endeavouring to beat down the price of it, it got into other hands'. However, More had not then visited Barnborough, and his later account is perhaps to be preferred. By either account, it is possible that 'Lady Gerrard' was kin to the More family.

belonging to Mr. [left blank] who left it in a house near Lime Street, Lond. a fire accidentally happening near the place. it was remov'd in a hurry, & carried to Cuttlers Hall . . . there being hung up severall years. the owner still living much reduced. & the *Clerk* of that Company. (Mr. Cuttel or Cotten) having got much wealth. married his daughter to Sir John Tyrrell of Essex & he prevailld with the Company who had no right to the picture, to let him remove it to Sir Johns house. where it now remains & the owner is not able to recover it.[1]

From the Tyrrell family it passed to the Petres of Thorndon and Ingatestone, who kept it until 1950.

This version is of slight importance as a representation of the central figure. The heavy moustache betrays it at once; further, the face is bloated and coarse, a weakening to be observed in the features of other members of the family as here depicted. That the fault lay rather in the inferior skill of the artist than in any defects of his model is confirmed by the omission of difficult detail. The work on the buffet and the diamond-paned window on the right, so intricate in the Nostell version, are instances of deliberate suppression in the Chelsea copy. The clock, though difficult to distinguish, appears to bear two hands, which would not have been possible for such a piece in the sixteenth century. The dog has changed position, being now at Sir John More's feet; and, more remarkably, it has changed breed. Altogether, it is a far cry from Locky, and farther still from Holbein, of whose original it is, nonetheless, the last and most debased copy of copies.

[1] *Notebooks*, II, 76.

8. THE ORDER OF THE HOLBEIN VERSIONS

Only the paintings and drawings described above can safely be described as 'by' or 'after' Holbein: the likenesses that follow, close or far as they may be from the Holbein likeness, have no immediate connection with any portrait known to have been painted or drawn by Holbein. Holbein, we know, executed two drawings and a portrait in oils of More alone, and a drawing and a life-size painting of More's family: miniatures, medals and engravings, however close in detail or in time they may be to Holbein's originals, cannot have the authenticity which can safely be ascribed to the pictures with which we have dealt so far. It is at this point, therefore, that it becomes necessary to consider the order, or at any rate a possible sequence, in which these likenesses were painted or drawn.

Hitherto this question has not been given much attention. The reason for this, unexpectedly, lies in the fact that the year of More's birth was for a long time the subject of much controversy. A misreading of John More's note of the birth of his son[1] led to the presumption that More was born in February 1477, and that therefore, since Holbein only reached England late in 1526 and More passed out of his 'fiftieth year'—the age indicated on the Basel sketch—in February 1527, the family group must have been painted first. The difficulty, then, of assuming that Holbein could have completed so large a work so soon after his arrival in England exercised the principal attention of scholars. But in 1935 Chambers demonstrated beyond doubt that More was born in 1478, and that therefore the dates on the family group portrait could safely indicate a date of April 1527.[2] The question of priority thus cannot be so simply decided, and we must turn back to the pictures themselves.

The evidence comes from six separate sources: the two Windsor drawings, the Frick version (from which the Lothian and other versions seem to derive), the Bedford version (which differs from the Frick in some respects, and with which the version once in the collection of Richard Tayloors and other versions seem to be related), the Basel Sketch, and Locky's copies of the family group, of which the Nostell version is perhaps the best. Now the best starting point in evaluating these sources is the second Windsor drawing. The irregularity, the physical impossibility, of certain features, corrected in the other versions, lend weight to the conjecture that this was Holbein's first sketch from the life. It will be remembered also that this drawing is pounced, or pricked, for transfer, the common method by which a drawing was transferred and used as a cartoon for the preliminary stages of a painting.

---

[1] In Trinity College, Cambridge, MS. O.2.21. See *Notes and Queries*, 4th Series, II (1868), pp. 365, 422, 449.
[2] R. W. Chambers, *Thomas More*, pp. 48–9, 219–20.

In the first half of 1952 the Frick version was very carefully cleaned and renovated by Mr William Suhr, Technical Consultant to the Frick collection. During the cleaning, the old discoloured restoration along the crack in the face (see fig. 3) was removed. The operation was carefully described and illustrated in a report to the Frick Trustees, which detailed the condition of the painting before and at several stages during the process. X-radiographs were taken which revealed a first image, subsequently altered and corrected, which differs from the first painting. The size and placing of the cap, the treatment of the cloth at the neck beneath the crossing of the fur collar, and—most important—the rendering of the features, in particular the eyes, all differ: and they differ in the same way that the second Windsor drawing differs from the finished portrait now in the Frick collection. It is difficult to avoid the conclusion that these alterations to the under-painting are only explicable in terms of correction and improvement made by the original artist, Holbein, himself as he built up the painting.[1]

From the virtual certainty that the second Windsor drawing is Holbein's first sketch, and that the Frick version is his first and original painting from it, we pass to a consideration of the other four likenesses. A close consideration of the features there depicted shews a number of minute alterations from what now may be fairly considered the authentic version. Three of these merit further attention. The most obvious is the treatment of the hair shewn emerging from under More's cap at his right temple: in the authentic version the strands nearest the cheek curl outwards; in the other versions they curl back, following the line of the cap. Secondly, the line of the bridge of the nose, broken in the authentic version, is obscure in the first Windsor drawing and the Basel Sketch, but is even and slightly curved in the Bedford and Locky versions. Finally, the line of the right eyebrow, distinctly broken in the authentic version and in the Basel Sketch, is obscure in the first Windsor drawing, and smoothed out in the Bedford and Locky versions. Now the smoothing out of irregularities is a characteristic of copying (another, the elongation of prominent features, is clearly perceptible in the Locky versions), and it is safe to express the opinion that the variations visible in the other four versions differ from the two with the greatest claims to authenticity in the way in which copies might be expected to differ from an original. A further conjecture—based on far less certainty—might be offered that the second Windsor drawing and the Basel Sketch, with which it might perhaps have been possible to group the original of the family group portrait, represent a second stage; and that the Bedford single portrait and the Locky versions are a later stage, though a sharp differentiation must be made between the two, which derive from different sources.

It is possible, too, that a link in the sequence may still be missing. The recent exhibition at the National Portrait Gallery clearly demonstrated the technique used by Holbein to construct his equally large later works, the destroyed Whitehall fresco and the group portrait of Henry VIII and the Barber Surgeons. It is tempting to suppose that Holbein may, perhaps for the first time, have used a similar technique in 1527. If so, it would be necessary

---

[1] An account of this inspection is promised for publication by Mr H. D. M. Grier, Assistant Director of the Collection, who kindly permits this anticipatory mention.

to assume the existence of a cartoon (now vanished) built up of full-size figures drawn in outline, cut out and pasted together in a composition which could be pricked directly on to the canvas or cloth on which the final picture was painted. Some evidence of its existence, however, may be found in the fact that among the drawings of the family at Windsor only that of More himself is pounced, to be used (it may now be safely said) for the single portrait. Moreover, as might be expected, no comparable portraits in oil of the other members of the family are known, based on the un-pounced drawings. But if Holbein needed a cartoon for the single portrait, he would need it far more for the larger group; it may then be inferred, since the other drawings of the family shew no signs of pricking, that if he used them at all for the group portrait, it was only to trace the outlines on to another sheet of paper. The process of extending such an outline tracing to full length, and the combination of all the figures, might well—paper being limited in size—have necessitated the 'collage' technique. Mr Piper suggests that the Basel sketch may be further evidence of the existence of the big cartoon. 'The character of this, at once so detailed and so schematic, is not that of a preparatory study', he writes; the detail, the fine line and almost complete absence of shading find a parallel in Holbein's work in the cartoon for the Whitehall fresco, which also shews signs of last-minute changes in the composition. That the large cartoon should have disappeared is not surprising; chance alone has preserved the Chatsworth and Barber-Surgeons cartoons. Only the finished painting could have revealed whether it ever did exist.[1]

If, then, any guess about the order of the earliest portraits of More is admissible, it might be this. First of all, Holbein did a head and shoulders sketch from the life in which, perhaps because More moved during the sitting, there were some inaccuracies (the second Windsor drawing). He then executed a half-length portrait in oils, in which the inaccuracies were put right (the Frick version). Next, there is the family group portrait, for which the first Windsor drawing may have been a secondary study and for which other studies exist, and of which the Basel Sketch represents a report of work in progress, possibly at the point when Holbein was transferring a full-scale composite cartoon to the surface of the surface of the group portrait. The Bedford version and the Locky copies of the family group are a subsequent stage. But—and it is a very large but—positive evidence of any kind extends only as far as the first two likenesses here considered. The connection between these and the other—second—group, and individually between these four versions is, to say the least, tenuous. It is, however, possible to say that in all these versions the authority of Holbein can be traced, an authority which lasted through centuries when the originals were lost from view, to be vindicated three hundred years later when the revival of interest in More demanded an authentic likeness.

[1] See Roy Strong, *The Burlington Magazine*, CV (1963), pp. 4–14, and David Piper, *loc. cit.*

9. THE MINIATURES

THERE are three miniature portraits of More, all good likenesses (of the Holbein image) and all of early date. All have been, at one time or another, attributed to Holbein, but it seems probable that the final proof of authenticity will always be lacking.[1] There is, moreover, a circumstance first recorded in van Mander's biography of Holbein, which must give pause to those who ascribe any of the three to Holbein. Van Mander notes that the painter did not practise the art of 'limning' until he entered the service of Henry VIII; his teacher then was 'the painter Lukas', clearly Luke Horenbout who was an already distinguished 'limner' in the King's service. If this was so, the earliest date for any Holbein miniature must be after 1532, during which year Holbein, although he was in England for the latter part of it, was not in the King's service.[2] Thus, there was little time for Holbein to perfect himself in the art of miniature painting before More was committed to the Tower in 1534. Lastly, it is to be noted that the majority of those miniatures which are confidently given to Holbein all date from the last years of his life.

Against this, however, may be set a number of differences between the 'miniature' portrait, and the likeness recorded in 1527, in the single portrait and in the group. In several points—the straighter nose, the lock of hair at the temple flicked back, the SS collar with the letter reversed—the miniatures resemble the latter: there is, however, a suggestion of age and sadness, a drawn look about the set of the jaw, which befits him who had resigned the chancellorship on 16 May 1532 and was rapidly falling from high office; the lock of hair, too, is perceptibly grey.[3] Lastly, there are a pair of miniatures of William and Margaret Roper, now in New York, which are accepted by Dr Ganz[4] as the authentic work of Holbein, and are certainly of considerable quality. Both have the ages of the sitters inscribed on them, and the miniatures can thus be accurately dated to 1536, the fifteenth anniversary of their marriage. So it is not impossible that Holbein, if indeed he painted miniatures of More's daughter and son-in-law a year after his death, could have earlier done the same for More.

If, however, Holbein did paint a miniature of More, that he painted a number is very unlikely. Accordingly, it may be prudent to conclude that the minatures are copies of a Holbein original, or of a miniature by another near-contemporary painter.

[1] None of them is included among those listed as certainly Holbein's work in the most authoritative survey of his miniatures yet published (Carl Winter, *Burlington Magazine*, LXXXIII (1943), pp. 266–9).

[2] The Household accounts for the years 1533–7 are lost, so it is not until 1538 that any record of Holbein's employment by Henry VIII is known.

[3] The cap is flatter and elongated, an alteration caused, in all probability, by the adaptation of the portrait to a circular or oval frame.

[4] Paul Ganz: *The Paintings of Hans Holbein*, London: 1950, p. 258.

101:*13*   Of the three, the best is that now in Lincoln's Inn. It may well be the original, for it first came to light in the possession of the Quicke family, and thus conceivably belonged to Margaret Roper with whose family the Quickes were related by marriage, a connection dating from the sixteenth century. It was bought by J. Pierpont Morgan in 1905, and thirty years later Sir Felix Cassell acquired it at the Pierpont Morgan sale at Christie's and presented it to Lincoln's Inn. The ascription to Holbein, in this case, is very early indeed. On the reverse —it is painted on vellum mounted on a card—is inscribed the one word 'Holbein' in a sixteenth century hand. There was also a piece of paper attached to its original frame on which, 'in a script of the early Stuart period',[1] was written the names of the subject and artist. A further point in favour of this ascription is the background of the miniature, which is a plain pale blue; though used by other painters, this style is found in all the miniatures certainly attributed to Holbein. But its exact status is likely to remain the subject of controversy. It can at least be said that it is a near-contemporary work, certainly pre-1550. If it is not by Holbein, it was perhaps executed by the same skilled hand (almost certainly Luke Horenbout) responsible for a group of miniatures of first quality produced during this period, with which, indeed, it has very close stylistic and technical affinities.[2]

102:*11*   A second early miniature of some, but not equal, quality is now in the Edward B. Greene collection of the Cleveland Museum of Art, Ohio. The portrait bears a very close resemblance to the Lincoln's Inn miniature, but the characteristics of age are rather more accentuated: the cheekbones are slightly more prominent, and the white hair more noticeable. It is harder to connect it with Holbein, if only because it is painted in oil on wood, whereas all his known miniatures are in watercolour on vellum, paper or card. Its provenance is only recorded as far as 1957, when it was acquired for the Museum.

108   It is, however, interesting to note that Abraham Van der Doort, in his catalogue of Charles I's pictures made between 1637 and 1640, attributes to Holbein a small head of More on wood which was kept in the Cabinet Room, where some of the best of the royal collection and all the miniatures were kept. It is mentioned in three of Van der Doort's drafts, most fully in the 'fair copy' now at Windsor.[3] Its provenance is there recorded as 'given to your Matie by Sir Henry Fanchurch', and described as

in a round tourn'd of one peece of wood and ye frame about it whited and gilded, whereupon the Picture painted is of Sr. Tho: Moore in a black Capp and furr'd gowne with redd sleeves painted upon the wrong lighte.

[1] Arthur Chamberlain, *Hans Holbein*, London 1913, i. 307.

[2] This miniature has been frequently reproduced. Some confusion has been caused by the fact that some reproductions are in reverse, looking left instead of right. A further source of confusion has been the change of frame; early reproductions show it in a plain round wooden frame, but this was changed during Morgan's ownership for an enamelled metal one. The *Bulletin of the Cleveland Museum of Art* (April 1959, pp. 54 and 57) illustrates it twice in the two different frames as two different pictures. For a discussion and reproductions of the group of miniatures now convincingly attributed to Horenbout, see G. Reynolds 'Portrait Miniatures', in *The Tudor Period* (Connoisseur Period Guides, ed. R. Edwards and L. G. G. Ramsey, 1956), pp. 127 ff.

[3] O. Millar, *A. Van der Doort's Catalogue of the Collections of Charles I*, Walpole Society, vol. XXXVII (1960), pp. 85, 191, 210.

The diameter is given as four inches, a fact which precludes the possibility that it may be identified with the Cleveland miniature, unless, and it is very unlikely, the dimensions given by Van der Doort include the frame. It is mentioned again in similar terms in another copy in the Victoria and Albert Museum, but the third description, in Van der Doort's 'rough draft' in the Bodleian Library, provides more details:

item inde kabinet rom de lute had auff tomas mor wij wer qijt dikat a gratadel spil tu rakoffer de sam terfor is wel wort

This may perhaps be interpreted as indicating that the little head of More by Holbein which was quite decayed and a great deal spoiled would be well worth restoring. Whether in fact it was restored is not recorded, but the picture was listed in September 1649 in the valuations of the royal collection, in which each item was appraised with a view to possible sale:

5. Sr. Thomas Moores Picture at ——— 20li — s — d.[1]

It remained unsold for some time, and M. de Bordeaux, Cardinal Mazarin's agent in London, noted it ('5 Le tableau de Thomas Morus') among the pictures in the royal collection in one of the lists which he sent to Paris; it was then at Somerset House.[2] Eventually, however, it was sold:

5: Sr. Tho: More   0020

appears in a long list of pictures, dated 23 October 1651, sold to 'George Greene and others.'[3]

It was not lost to the royal collection for long. Even before the Restoration, an Act of Parliament was passed for the recovery of the King's property, under which commissioners were appointed for that purpose. Among these was Colonel William Hawley, whose special task was to retrieve the King's pictures. He kept a journal of his attempts which (its earlier pages, at any rate) records those he was able to get back, and in his second list appears the picture of Sir Thomas More.[4] It returned to its old place with the other miniatures, and is listed in the catalogue drawn up c. 1666–7 among those in the King's Closet at Whitehall as:

447 Holbin Sr Thomas Moore. I(n) a round guilt frame.[5]

The diameter is again given as four inches, a nice confirmation that it is the same picture as that listed by Van der Doort. It appears finally in the inventory of James II's pictures, drawn up by William Chiffinch, and dated 16 February 1688 (o.s.), in the second section which, though not described as such, is clearly a catalogue of the pictures in the King's Closet:

54 By Holbein A head of Sr Thomas Moore.[6]

[1] Public Record Office, LR2, 124, f 161v. I owe this, and the following references, to Mr Oliver Millar.
[2] G. J. de Cosnac, *Les Richesses du Palais Mazarin* (Paris, 1884), p. 414.
[3] Public Record Office, SP. 29/447, 24.1.   [4] British Museum, Add. MS. 17916, f7v.
[5] MS Inventory of Charles II's pictures at Whitehall and Hampton Court, in the Office of the Surveyor of the Queen's Pictures.
[6] British Museum, Harl MS. 1890, f. 64v.

Thereafter, it disappears. It is a sadly plausible conjecture that it may have been lost in the Whitehall fire in 1697/8; on the other hand, the inventories of the royal pictures of the early eighteenth century are not so detailed as those of the late seventeenth, and it may have gone at a later date.

Another picture known to have existed in the seventeenth century was probably of a similar type. On 15 February 1649 (o.s.), John Evelyn visited Sir William Ducy, as recorded in his diary:

> Sir William *Ducy* shewd me some excellent things in Miniature, & in Oyle of *Holbeins* Sir Tho: Mores head.[1]

It is not wholly clear from this description that the head of More was in fact a miniature, but it seems unlikely that a *head* could be anything else.

The third miniature is in the collection of the Duke of Buccleuch. It is executed in oil, probably on gesso, on an oval silver plaque. It is an early copy of the miniature portrait, certainly no later than the seventeenth century. Nothing is known of its history before 1857 when it was exhibited at Manchester: it too has been attributed to Holbein, notably by Mr Dudley Heath,[2] but with rather less probability than the other two miniatures.[3]

This miniature, like the other two, may have been painted for family reasons. Or again, it may have been made to satisfy the demands of friends or literary acquaintances or admirers. Their love of More's writings and, indeed, the spirit of tolerance and humanity for which he stood, could not have been openly expressed between 1535 and 1553. But it is not unlikely that his trial and martyrdom provided an opportunity for copyists to sell miniature portraits, then still a novel and probably fashionable medium of commemoration. Of this, the twin miniatures of the Ropers may perhaps be an example. Queen Mary's reign may have encouraged the production of further copies, although it needs to be said that the great folio edition of More's works which William Rastell edited and John Cawood and others published in 1557 contains no engraving of the author. The reason for this, however, can only have been the shortage of competent craftsmen-engravers: London had excellent painters and miniaturists but no fine engravers upon wood and none on copper. As will be seen, it was on the Continent that the first portraits in these media were produced.

If no engravings of More were made in London between 1553 and 1559, paintings of him now attributed to Holbein, and others that have no attribution, may have been made at this period. Some may be among those recorded in inventories or as passing through the saleroom. Indeed, before concluding this account of the miniatures, mention must be made of one of the most tantalizing of all these records, a note made by Vertue on his first visit to the Mores of Barnborough in 1728[4] of

---

[1] John Evelyn, *Diary*, ed. E. S. de Beer (Oxford, 1955), ii, p. 549.

[2] The *Connoisseur*, vol. XVIII, No. 71 (1907), where it is reproduced in colour.

[3] A further account will be found in H. A. Kennedy, *Early English Portrait Miniatures in the collection of the Duke of Buccleuch* (London, 1917), p. 29 (pl. X). An earlier reproduction, in the catalogue of the Burlington Fine Arts Club Exhibition of Early English Portraiture (1909), is in fact of the Lincoln's Inn miniature.

[4] *Notebooks*, II, 75.

a George in Gold enamell'd. within which (as a case or relickquary) is in small by holben the picture   108
of S^r. Tho More in Water Colours, faded.

Now this cannot be the same as any of the known miniatures. Only the Lincoln's Inn miniature could be described as in 'watercolours', and it is known to have been in a different
frame at least as early as the seventeenth century; moreover, if in the possession of any
branch of More's descendants, it must have been on the Roper side of the family. The
miniature 'in a George in Gold'—and possibly other contemporary portraits of More—
may still be hidden somewhere and may some time be discovered and recognized.

10. THE BRONZE MEDALLION

HE works just described above constitute the recognized paintings, drawings and miniatures that are loosely described as 'after Holbein'. One or other original provided the data for a likeness of More which was accepted among craftsmen as authentic; and this was the basis for the copies which, with individual differences, have satisfied those who wished to acquire such a likeness, in More's lifetime and since. Hitherto, moreover, we have been covering ground which has never ceased to be of interest to the *cognoscenti*, and which therefore has been to some extent, if imperfectly, documented throughout the intervening years. The subsequent portraiture of More, however, much of which differs very considerably from the image to which we have grown accustomed, has been little studied, and if connections are to be made and a line of development traced, it can only be from inspection of the portraits themselves: there is no written evidence.

301:14–15 But there is one important likeness that may help to bridge the gap, which has not been described before in this connection. This is a unique bronze medallion now in the British Museum, which cannot be dated much after 1550, and may possibly be earlier. It is first known, late in the eighteenth century, in the notable collection, famous also for its incunabula on vellum, of the Yorkshire baronet Sir Mark Masterman Sykes.[1] From thence it passed to Edward Hawkins, F.R.S.,[2] a controversial figure who compiled the first catalogue of the historical medals at the Museum. As the illustration shews, it bears a considerable similarity to the miniatures, but it is a course and rough-cast affair, unlike the portrait-medallions executed by Antonio Pisano, called Pisanello (*c.* 1380–*c.* 1455), the Veronese medallist, for the commemoration of great contemporaries, which were the original models for the circular miniatures already discussed. However, it is this roughness and the characteristic distortion of cap and nose, which suggest the early date. It bears a close resemblance to the work of the group of Flemish and German medallists, which includes Hans Daucher, Joachim Forster, Christoph Weiditz and Hans Schwarz, all of whom were working about this time. After 1550, the style of such medallions alters noticeably: the relief is shallower, the detail more fine.

It is obvious that no conjecture about the identity of the artist is likely to receive confirmation. Nevertheless, there is a possibility which should be mentioned here. Jan Everardi,

---

[1] (1771–1823). During his ownership, an engraving was made, based on the medallion, an example of which is to be found in the Department of Prints and Drawings in the British Museum.

[2] (1780–1867), Keeper of Antiquities at the British Museum from 1826 to 1860. His catalogue, which the Trustees of the Museum refused to publish on account of the strong Protestant and Tory views expressed in it, eventually appeared in 1885, edited by A. W. Franks and H. A. Grueber, as *Medallic Illustrations of the History of Great Britain and Ireland*.

better known as Joannes Secundus, is chiefly famous for his *Basiae*, a collection of amatory verse frequently reprinted and very popular right down to the end of the eighteenth century. He also wrote an *Epitaphium* and a longer elegy, *Naenia*, on the death of Thomas More. And lastly, he was a not undistinguished amateur medallist. Altogether, he was a man of many talents, cut short untimely. Born at the Hague in 1511, the son of a famous lawyer, he first found fame at the court of Margaret of Austria at Malines. In 1529, he executed his first medal, a portrait of his father. Later he entered the service of Charles V, and as his poet laureate accompanied the Emperor on his expedition to Tunis in the summer of 1535. Prevented by a fever from crossing to Africa, he declined and died on 24 September in the following year at the abbey of St Amand in Tournai. Before he died, however, he finished his poem on the death of More, which had evidently moved him deeply. His indignation against the power that had destroyed More was so violently expressed that the poems were first circulated anonymously, and on their first appearance in print in the month of the poet's death were mistakenly attributed to Erasmus. When the official edition of his works was printed 1541, a more correct text was published, but with certain passages omitted, *quod in principes quosdam acerbius dicta viderentur*, according to the editors, the poet's two surviving brothers.[1] Whether Secundus had known More living is not clear; it seems unlikely, but, as will be seen, he was well acquainted with More's friends at Louvain.

His talents as a medallist were first revealed by the Flemish scholar Kits in 1838; other works were added to his *œuvre*, and a definitive account was published at the end of the century by Dr Julien Simonis.[2] In it he listed no fewer than eighteen medals which he attributed to Secundus, among them portraits of More's old friends Peter Gilles and—a very fine example—Erasmus. There is considerable variation in style in the eighteen medals,[3] as may be expected in the work of an amateur. The differences are probably accentuated by the fact that most of the known specimens are known only in later casts. Some, however, are sufficiently rough in appearance to bear comparison with our medallion. The possibility that Secundus is responsible for it too can only remain a possibility, but none the less interesting for that.

Lastly, a word must be said about the design on the reverse of the medallion, which has its own interest, and which, as will be seen, recurs in a most unexpected way.

This shews a newly felled tree, possibly the palm which signifies martyrdom, with the axe still embedded in the stump, and the legend SVAVIVS OLET.[4] This gives us a clue to the imagery: as the sap of a tree cut down in its prime smells sweeter, so the blood of

[1] His epitaph was reprinted in several later lives of More, among them Stapleton's and Regi's (see below, pp. 42–3, 61 and 64).

[2] *L'Art du Medailleur en Belgique* (Brussels, 1900), pp. 35–92.

[3] Habich, in his monumental *Die deutsche Medailleure*, has disproved some of Simonis's attributions, and gives some of them to Weiditz, though none of those mentioned above. Some of Weiditz's work resembles the present medallion, and it is interesting to note that Habich emphasizes the influence of Holbein in his later medals.

[4] This motto, which might seem to be common enough, does not appear in any of the standard manuals of emblemology and devices. *Suaviter olet* was the motto of Henri de Bourbon, Duc de Montpensier and grandfather of Madame de Montpensier, a fact of little relevance to the present inquiry.

martyrs is dearer in the sight of God. To be precise, this is the first representation of More as the martyr he became on 6 July 1535 and not merely as the chancellor he had ceased to be on 16 May 1532. The importance of this fact needs no emphasis. Hitherto, the first steps toward the recognition of More as a martyr for religion have been supposed to be taken at the time of the reform of the English College at Rome about 1579–83, a movement which will concern us later. This medallion shows, however, that there was, perhaps among the English refugees from Henrican persecution in the Low Countries, one to whom More was already a martyr to be acknowledged and celebrated.

Figure 11. The miniature in the
Cleveland Museum of Art, Ohio (102)

Figure 12. John Fowler's woodcut,
1568 (201)

ERRATUM

The captions of Figures 11 and 13 have been transposed.   The top left
illustration is of the Lincoln's Inn miniature ; the centre illustration is
of the miniature in the Cleveland Museum of Art, Ohio.

n's Inn (101)

Figures 14 and 15. Bronze medallion,
obverse and reverse (301)

4+

Figure 16 *above*. Woodcut, shewing the execution of
More, in *Ein Anzaygung*, 1536 (601)

Figure 17 *right*. Detail of the engraving by Circignani,
in *Ecclesiae Anglicanae Trophaea*, 1584 (604)

Figure 18. The execution of More, probably by Antoine Caron, *c.* 1590 (606)

Part Two

THE LATER IMAGE

1. INTRODUCTION

The future portraits of More differ in many ways from those described hitherto. During his lifetime he had numerous friends who had gathered round him when he was at the height of his prestige, who, as well as the members of his family, might want to have his portrait. For them, a *likeness*, something from which they could recapture a familiar image, was essential; thus, the features which have remained constant with little variation in all the portraits so far noticed must be, as near as may be, the features of More as his friends knew him. From now on the purpose of portraiture changes completely. The paintings and engravings of the next 150 years show the chancellor, the scholar, the martyr; they are not designed to recall a face known to friends. It is not surprising, then, that they differ.

There is another practical reason for the change. When More resigned the chancellorship in May 1532, there was less occasion to pay respect to the King's former friend, the holder of the highest offices of the realm. When he was in disfavour his books were not reprinted in London and, when he was executed, there could be no provision of a portrait to serve as a frontispiece or illustration to any eulogy that might have been composed by his family or friends. They must now keep out of harm's way, and any portraits they possess are inaccessible, doubly so, since anything of the kind would now need to be produced abroad. The beheading of a statesman who had fallen out of Henry's favour entailed the execration of his name. No public expression of sympathy with him was possible. There was to be no propaganda in his behalf in all England. More's portraits remained hidden in the privacy of personal possession, although some inevitably went abroad, where the name and fame of More were now cherished to an increasing degree; there they may have served as models for some of the portraits which appeared in later years, made by artists who had never seen More when living, and who, so far as they intended a likeness at all, were apt to misconstrue their original.

The former chancellor had not been a subject for continental artists in his lifetime, except for the figures cut by Ambrose Holbein in 1518 for Froben's edition of *Utopia*, long before Hans Holbein met the author of the book. More's *Utopia* remained one of the most popular books in Europe, so much so that even in Elizabethan England the word denoted an ideal or imaginary political state. Thus Robert Cecil, the Queen's principal secretary of state, can reject Tyrone's conditions for peace in Ireland with the word 'Yewtopia'; and that was the end of them. Few English authors maintained their place so firmly in the international booksellers' lists and the printers' contracts for so long and in so many foreign centres. English printing was, however, in no condition to lavish upon him the frontispieces and cuts, with verses beneath, for the benefit of their public. They came, therefore, from Antwerp, Louvain, Frankfurt, Paris. The English trade had begun late and was hindered by laws that limited the practice of the art to London and the two universities. In 1586 Elizabeth, by decree of the Star Chamber, superseded previous restrictions by a comprehensive system of supervision which lasted until 1637. This was strict enough; yet in 1599 the authorities ordered that 'no English histories be printed except those allowed by the Council'. Under the Star Chamber it was unlikely that the name, fame and portraiture of More should flourish in his own country.

The situation was different elsewhere. In certain continental centres printing was freer and artists and engravers were encouraged. In the second half of the sixteenth century engraved portraiture was a regular branch of publishing. Portfolios of the famous personalities, with or without biographies, were fashionable. In the Low Countries, particularly, the arts of engraving on wood and copper flourished. The violence of controversy and the passion of nationalism stimulated to a degree, never before experienced, the portrayal of contemporary personalities. The heads of monarchs and royal personages had been painted in the Middle Ages, and barons after them. Now for the first time in history, living writers, theologians and philosophers were 'news', with the world on the brink of the invention of the periodical newspaper. The exponents of the new religion were quick to seize the propaganda value of pictures of their leaders to supplant pictures of the saints. Engravers were quick to seize the opportunity presented by such a complex of emotions and creeds, to put forth numerous single prints of portraits of those whom they advertised as the most famous, the most erudite, and so on.

Hence the time was, and would remain, propitious for the portrait of one who had described an ideal commonwealth, who had written on theology with philosophy, who had risen to the highest position in his country. Few could compete with the variety of attractions that More offered to his generation and the next. Many prints of his figure were published; a number survive; some can be dated; few are placeable in their appropriate context. Even their place of origin cannot always be ascertained and the special intention, apart from making a profit, that impelled the printing of certain plates cannot be ascertained with certainty. The general motive has already been indicated: there was a public for portraits of men of name and fame. And at that time when *Utopia* was being read and re-read More's portrait would be in demand. Prints not necessarily forming part of a book carried verses beneath them. The sale of such single prints was conducted by the booksellers, who would offer the purchaser of More's works a portrait which the binder would insert as a frontispiece, i.e. where one was not included by the printer. There are instances of apocryphal portraits of More being bound into sets of his collected works.

This is the new background against which we must survey the printed portraiture of More. It will be found that the majority are engravings, and that these, with some of the paintings, fall into fairly definite groups, although there are some interesting exceptions.

2. THE EXECUTION OF MORE

THE first of these groups in point of time is the relatively small number of representations of the execution of More. These were produced first for the general purpose of illustrating the news, which had shocked all Europe, of More's death, and later for the more particular purpose of depicting More as a martyr, to further the Catholic cause.

John Fisher, Bishop of Rochester, had been destroyed on 22 June 1535. More's turn came on 6 July. By the royal will the former chancellor was beheaded early in the morning without leave to make the customary speech from the scaffold. He would have been a bold artist to make public a drawing of that scene. That unsympathetic if vivid recorder, the chronicler Edward Hall, set down an account which is important as having been put on paper years before Roper decided to write his memoir. Hall was under-sheriff at the time, and was in a position to know the facts; his *Chronicle* was published in 1542. Relevant to our purpose is his statement that 'he [More] having a great gray beard, striked out his beard and said to the executioner: "I pray you let me lay my beard over the block lest ye should cut it".' Doubtless More had ceased to shave when he first went to the Tower. Stapleton, in *Tres Thomae* (Douai, 1588), recounting More's last hours, adds the further detail that he was wearing a plain frieze garment and carrying a red cross in his hand.[1]

The first representation appeared, in fact, in a German translation of the account of More's death, generally known by its Latin title *Expositio Fidelis de Morte D. Thomae Mori*, which spread like wild-fire on the Continent in the months following his execution.[2] *Ein glaubwirdige Anzaygung des Tods Herrn Thome Mori* lacks place and printer's name, but it was probably printed in Augsburg; it came out in 1536. It contains two wood-cuts; both shew More as wearing a long plain garment and with a beard kneeling at the block. The backgrounds and the other figures are purely conventional; indeed it is possible that both are 'stock blocks', which might be used for any similar publication. However, they are competently and vigorously done and may have been specially engraved for this particular edition. 601:*16*

There is in the British Museum a manuscript which appears to be based to some extent on the *Expositio Fidelis*.[3] It was written by or for Odinet Godrand, president of the Parliament

[1] That the royal policy was to have the former chancellor's aspect rendered detestable was clear from the refusal to except his head from the customary parboiling, which might prevent the trouble which had ensued when Fisher's head had been exposed, seeming 'as though it had been alive, looking upon the people coming into London' until they began to talk of a miracle. Such was the power of a man's face.

[2] For further information on this, and of Erasmus's connection with it, the reader is referred to Professor H. de Vocht's *Acta Thomae Mori* (Louvain, 1947) and J. D. M. Derrett in the Bulletin of the Institute of Historical Research, XXXIII (1960), pp. 202–23.

[3] Add MS. 28786; see *Letters and Papers, Foreign and Domestic, of the Reign of Henry VIII*, vol. viii, no. 997.

of Burgundy, for the use of his father. Godrand died in 1581, so the manuscript must have been written before then. On the first page of the main text, there is a highly coloured and fanciful representation of More's execution. He is shown beardless, his hands together in prayer, in a large red cloak which falls to the ground, on which a flat black cap is lying. The executioner is dressed in puffed breeches and has a long curling feather in his hat; to the right there is a tree; to the left, Henry, fierce-featured and clad in a blue cloak, is giving the signal. The scene takes place in a green meadow, with a range of blue hills in the background. Vivid though it is, the miniature has clearly no relation to any portrait of More based on reality.

In 1584 there appeared an etching which bears some resemblance to the wood-cuts of 1536. It is not, however, a casual production for an ephemeral pamphlet. It appeared in Rome, at the time, mentioned before, when the English College was re-orientated to the Mission to England, and in a work privileged by the Pope. The cult of the English men and women who suffered the extreme penalty for maintaining the supremacy of the see of Peter was first given formal sanction under Gregory XIII (1572–85). That pope, shortly before his death, conceded that relics of the English martyrs could, in default of others, serve for the consecration of altars. Also, he permitted the *Te Deum* to be publicly sung on the receipt of the news of the execution of the members of the English College who volunteered for the mission. Finally, he permitted the college, whose founder he was, to place their portraits, with their names attached, in the chapel. And this was duly accomplished. These pictures, therefore, are of historical and documentary significance. They were the gifts to the college of George Gilbert, of whom more presently. While there he organized the series of paintings that Gregory XIII had authorized, probably at his personal persuasion. One of these shows the execution of More.

There is reason to accept the details of this picture as authentic; for, according to the Annual Letter of the English College, Gilbert was accompanied by 'a young relative of the illustrious martyr, Sir Thomas More, who had conferred many benefits on the Fathers of the Society of Jesus and the Catholic cause, and whose conduct among us proves that he is not unworthy of his sainted kinsman'. This young relative was Charles Basset, S.J., a son of James Basset who married Mary, one of the daughters of Margaret and William Roper, the Chancellor's daughter and son-in-law.

It is not unreasonable to suppose that Charles Basset possessed, or had access to, pictures and portraits of More such as were treasured by the family. The details of his personal appearance and of his demeanour during his last hours and execution continued to be cherished by his admirers. Fifty years afterwards one such account (several times reprinted in the ensuing century) was published, Thomas Stapleton's. He had industriously collected at first hand the materials for his *Tres Thomae* published at Douai in 1588, which includes the *Vita Thomae Mori* which was subsequently printed separately, as will be noted shortly. Stapleton here says that Margaret Giggs, the wife of John Clement, 'once shewed me a life-like image, made with great skill, of More going to the place of execution, and in accordance with that image I have described here his appearance and demeanour'.

42

More's personal appearance is thus delineated by Stapleton:

Not tall in stature, but well formed and of perfect proportions. His complexion tended to phlegmatic. In colour he was white and pale. Of joyous countenance, his expression was cheerful and amiable; yet his refined face was thoroughly in keeping with the responsible positions he held. His eyes were grey and somewhat small; although not brilliant they were kindly. His forehead was broad. His hair was straight and uncurled, in colour between dark and fair. His neck was short and thick. His hair was dressed after the manner of the nobility and gentry of that day. These details have been handed down to us by eye-witnesses.

It can hardly be doubted, therefore, that the image of More was thus remembered in this period, that is, within the life of his grandchildren. Basset, therefore, may in all likelihood have kept a portrait of the man and a picture of the scene of his execution. So when Gilbert, with the authority of Gregory XIII, arranged for a series of paintings for the English College, he may reasonably be presumed to have taken the trouble of ensuring the authenticity of the details where he had the opportunity. The scheme ranks as one of the most ambitious of all examples of the use of the pictorial element in propaganda. It was designed to inspire the students by the example of the martyrs of England.

It has been seen that these paintings were the gift of George Gilbert and it has been argued that the details were authentic where he had the opportunity to secure them, and that in respect of More he probably had access to the facts through Basset. In the work of propaganda by picture, Gilbert had the co-operation of William Good, S.J. (see p. 44). Basset died at Rheims in 1584.

George Gilbert (1555–83) was a convert from Puritanism. A man of serious purpose, he had early come under the tutelage of Dering, the East Anglian Protestant leader. In 1579 he was received into the Church by Robert Persons, S.J. He later joined the resistance association which brought over to England missionary priests to serve the Catholic laity, and guaranteed their material support. This association was given semi-official status and was blessed by Gregory XIII in 1580. As one of its leaders Gilbert ran great risks. As a constant companion of Persons, and Campion, he was pursued by the law. As a fugitive he crossed to Rouen and then went to Rheims. Finally, as an alumnus he entered the English College at Rome. He is a deserving subject for a modern biographer interested in the beginnings of the English Counter-Reformation. This man from Beaconsfield was as good at horse-riding, vaulting and fencing as he was with prayer, fasting and devotion. He was a character. His dialectical patronage of art alone marks him as an unusual type of layman. Before he died he had completed all arrangements for the frescoes and, towards the end of his life, Gilbert was received, as a scholastic, into the Society of Jesus, and died on 6 October 1583.

The paintings commissioned by Gilbert numbered some forty or more subjects, which ranged from the despatch to England by Saint Peter of Saint Joseph of Arimathaea to the martyrdom of Saint Alban, Saint Boniface and Saint Thomas of Canterbury. The Reformation subjects begin with the Carthusians and proceed to the priests, regulars and seculars, and laymen and women under Elizabeth. The painter, Niccolò Circignani (1519–90), was usually known as Il Pomarancio (from his birthplace near Volterra). He is the artist mentioned earlier in this account as, according to Roger North, happening to be 'coming by' when Henry VIII threw Holbein's portrait out of the window of the palace, when the news was brought of More's execution.

Il Pomarancio was an artist of some reputation. He was favoured by the Jesuits and by Gregory XIII, the pope who about the year 1575 created the English College out of the old medieval hospice. He was already esteemed for the frescoes of the martyrs he painted in the restored ancient church of S. Stefano Rotondo and for another set of frescoes he made for the German College newly founded by the Jesuits. Of both these considerable enterprises etchings, then a relatively new process, had been made and published in book form. Before Gilbert's death it had been decided to publish a similar book based on the frescoes in the English College with the help of another Jesuit, one from England.

A certain Fr Good, who had been in Poland from 1577 to 1580 on the mission begun by Peter Canisius, S.J., was active on behalf of Gilbert's scheme. The same Good had instructed him in the faith and fostered his vocation. William Good (1527–86) was one of those who left England at the beginning of Elizabeth's reign. He had been a Fellow of Corpus Christi, Oxford, in Queen Mary's time. In 1562 he joined the Society of Jesus and was one of the first Englishmen to do so. It may have been he who gave Gilbert the impetus to follow the example of Canisius in the exploitation of graphic art in the service of religion. Good had also been the moving spirit behind the book of etchings based on the frescoes painted by Il Pomarancio at S. Stefano Rotondo.

The printing of the book of the English frescoes was not finished until the year after Gilbert's death. *Ecclesiae Anglicanae Trophaea, sive Sanctorum Martyrum . . . qui Persecutionem . . . Mortem in Angliae subierunt Passiones Romae in Collegio Anglico per Nicolaum Circinianum depictae*, made its appearance in 1584. The engraving was the work of G. B. Cavalieri and the book was printed on the rolling press of Bartholomeo Grassi. There is no letterpress, except the licence to print. The name of the sponsor is given as Thomas Tretezo, canon of Santa Maria in Trastevere. He was a former cleric of the diocese of Poznan in Poland and a friend of Good's.

The book has the privilege of Gregory XIII, addressed to Bartholomeo Grassi, apparently well known in Rome as a publisher of etchings. On the whole it is a handsome production. The use of etching was relatively new and represents an interesting aspect of Jesuit innovation; for it is a much more rapid and much less expensive medium of illustration than the line-engraving that Canisius employed. The Society had shown its interest in typography in its early years. Shortly before his death in 1556, Ignatius Loyola secured a press for the Jesuit College in Rome. In 1556 the first practical typography in Arabic was executed there. Gregory XIII, too, was personally interested, perhaps directly inspired by the Jesuits.

The English *Trophaea* became of paramount documentary importance in 1798 when the College virtually ceased to exist and Pius VI was exiled. The sacking and pillaging destroyed the original frescoes and left the college in a state that required years for its restoration. The replicas to be seen there at the present time are based upon the etchings in the *Trophaea*.[1]

The book is folio size and comprises thirty-six plates, of which the last depicts Gregory XIII as founder of the English College, with Cardinal Buoncompagni as its protector and a number of alumni being prepared for the mission. Plate 27 is a composite picture, the important detail for our purpose being that of More, shewn at his execution, the detail being very much like the wood-cuts of the 1536 news letter. There is, however, a difference: whereas until this date More had been depicted as humanist and author, as chancellor or quondam chancellor, it was in 1584 solely as a martyr that he was memorialized on the walls of the English College and in the book of etchings.

604:17

A similar but inferior engraving is included for the first time in the 1592 edition of Richard Verstegan's *Theatrum Crudelitatum Haereticorum nostri Temporis* (Antwerp). It, too, is a composite picture, shewing the execution of Fisher and the Charterhouse monks at the same time, but the whole scene is so conventional in its delineation that it may be rated as a diagram rather than a picture. The work itself is a propagandist work, full of the excess of late sixteenth-century controversy. It does nothing to further More's cause. Indeed, it would seem that, already at the end of his own century, More's death and the circumstances of it were not remembered by a world habituated to savagery—where persecution was normal everywhere in every Christian sect that had the power. It was More's literary works that were commemorated, not the cause for which he died. Outside Rome there was no interest in More's martyrdom. Not only so, but Catholics themselves were forgetful of More's execution. There was a reason for this unmindfulness. Mary had reigned since and had acted upon the principle, held since the beginnings of Roman Emperor-worship, that dissent from the monarchical religion was treason. When Elizabeth came to the throne it was the turn of the Catholics to be persecuted. The sufferings of the Catholics after 1559 were not merely fresh in the memory of those living in 1592, but were contemporary and continuous. It was too late to attempt to give the Henrican martyrs, the Carthusians, Fisher and More, their deserved rank.

607

Mention must also be made of a remarkable painting in the Musée de Blois in France. It is a large panel by Antoine Caron, and it is dated, on grounds of costume, about 1590. It shews a bearded figure in a long gown being led to execution, which is seen taking place in the background; the procession is interrupted by a young woman who has cast herself at his feet, to the consternation of the guards. The latter are clad in what the sixteenth century imagined to be Roman armour; the whole picture is romantic in conception. A convincing case has been made out recently[2] that it represents the execution of More, the young woman being Margaret Roper, who, by her husband's account, broke through the

606:18

---

[1] It is perhaps germane to record here a picture noted by Sir George Scharf (S.S.B.114, p. 46), showing More in gown, skull-cap and beard, and inscribed B. THOMAS MORUS CUM AD PATIBULUM DUCERETUR. Scharf's note was made in 1887, from a photograph; the picture was then in the Barberini Palace in Rome. It seems possible that it was related to Pomarancio's picture; as described, it also seems to have resembled a miniature, to be described shortly.

[2] J. Ehrmann, *Burlington Magazine*, XCII (1950), p. 36.

guards to her father, as he was being taken back to the Tower after being sentenced. The purpose for which the picture was painted, however, remains a mystery.

The striking fact about all these different representations of More's execution is the close correspondence in detail, despite origins so different that copying is almost out of the question. Much, no doubt, of this similarity may be due to what may be called the 'convention of the subject matter'. Artists must frequently have been called upon to produce pictures of similar subjects, with very inadequate briefs to enable them to do so, and this undoubtedly accounts for some general similarity. But there is enough in the details to suggest that there was a common source, of which Margaret Clement's picture was no doubt an important example, being based on eye-witness record.

Another painting, which belongs to this group, is listed in an inventory (now in the Escorial) of the royal portrait collection.[1] It was drawn up for Philip II of Spain in 1587, and in it the subjects of the portrait are set out under various categories, that of More (as also one of Fisher) being recorded under 'beatos'. The More is said to have been copied from a picture originally in the possession of English Catholics at Rome—a suggestive detail—and depicted More *en el cadahalco*, in which detail it would appear to be unique. Another remarkable reference is contained in a manuscript catalogue, now in the Department of Prints and Drawings at the British Museum, of part of the collection of Sir Hans Sloane; it is a copy, made some time after the main Sloane catalogue of 1837, of an obviously eighteenth-century original, perhaps drawn up during Sloane's lifetime since it lists items not included in the Sloane bequest. One such—sadly—is

278. St. Thomas More in Crayons June 1535 by Hans *Holbein*

That Holbein should have been able to draw More a month before his execution is incredible, yet Vertue, who saw the drawing in 1713,[2] accepted the attribution; unless it can be found again, who can say?

Finally, there is a miniature,[3] attributed to Holbein and certainly of some quality, shewing a man, half-length, dressed in a plain robe, with a long beard, and carrying a red cross in his hand. All this might easily be dismissed, but for the fact that the face exhibits a remarkable resemblance to the Holbein likeness of More, which was demonstrably from the life. Conjecture dare go no further.

No further 'execution' pictures are known after the sixteenth century. Gilbert had close personal access to Gregory XIII, who was wont to consult him on English affairs, but after his death nothing of a formal nature seems to have been instituted. Only in 1612 was an inquiry begun by Urban VIII. A list of martyrs was drawn up by the Vicar Apostolic, Richard Smith, Bishop of Chalcedon, before his death in 1655; but the Civil War seems to have postponed any action by Rome, and much weakened the cult of More as martyr. Meanwhile, the world ranked him as the greatest scholar after Erasmus.

[1] The inventory is promised for publication by Dr Kurz, who kindly permits this reference.
[2] *Notebooks*, I, 32.
[3] In the collection of the Melander Shakespeare Society.

3. EARLY ENGRAVINGS

THE image depicted in the 'execution' pictures is far removed from those which derive, at however many removes, from the Holbein image. To delineate More as victim and martyr it was not necessary to achieve likeness of feature. The executioner, the block, and perhaps the beard were details enough to drive home the message. The portraits which now concern us are designed to shew More as author, scholar, or simply as a famous man of his age; for these some degree of likeness was more necessary. Nevertheless, it should be remembered that if the artist knew little of his subject's real appearance, it would not greatly concern him. The variations, then, which appear in the early engravings, while they may partly be derived from originals now lost of a different likeness of More, are at least as likely to be caused by the artist attempting to emphasize the scholar or the distinguished politician.

The first, however, is clearly based on a miniature; the fact that the subject is shewn looking left suggests that it may have been copied directly on to wood from a miniature such as those described above, which are all looking right. It is, in fact, the earliest known rendering of More's features in wood engraving, after the *Utopia* printed at Basel 201:*12* by Froben in 1518,[1] and appears at the end of the prefatory matter of his argument against Johann Bugenhagen (1485–1553), the Lutheran famous for the spread of that religion in North Germany and Denmark. Bugenhagen's (in Latin Pomeranus) propagandist tract addressed to the Church in England had been translated, and More's answer, *Epistola in qua non minus facete quam pie respondet literis Ioannis Pomerani, hominis inter Protestantes non obscuri*, was printed in 1568 by John Fowler at Louvain. The same block reappears in the preliminaries of *A Dialogue of Cumfort against Tribulation, made by . . . Sir Thomas More, sometime Lord Chancellor of England*. This latter text was printed at Antwerp 'Apud Ioannem Foulerum, Anglus' in 1573, twenty years after its original appearance in London at the press of Richard Tottell, in Queen Mary's time.

John Fowler was born at Bristol in 1537, became a scholar of Winchester in 1551–3 and proceeded to New College, Oxford. In 1559 he was one of the fifteen fellows who rejected the oath of supremacy to Elizabeth and was obliged to withdraw to Louvain where he opened a printing house about 1565 and continued in the trade until his death at Namur in 1579. He married Alice, daughter of More's secretary, John Harris, who is the young man added, probably at More's wish, to Holbein's group painting as rendered by Rowland

---

[1] The French translation of *Utopia* (1550) contains a lively but crude copy of the group in the garden; it also contains a cut of More writing in his study. The 1563 *Lucubrationes* contains a copy of the map with figures which first appeared in 1518.

Locky. Alice Harris may have possessed a copy, perhaps in miniature, of one or other of the existing portraits; or at least could have provided her husband with access to one. In any case, Fowler's cut is derived from Holbein, its oval shape being possibly caused by the need to adapt a circular original to the oblong form of a book page. The medallion is surrounded by the text THOMAS MORVS ANGLVS ANNO AETATIS 50, another link with Holbein, since it presumes an original of the year of Holbein's known paintings, 1527.

It is not to be compared with the earlier pictures. No doubt, however, it sufficiently satisfied the curiosity and piety of the modestly endowed folk for whom Fowler printed his pocket edition of the *Dialogue*. Prints of the block were sold separately and may be found, worked on finer paper; a specimen exists in the British Museum. Fowler has the excuse that he was not a professional printer or bookseller. He was clearly short of capital and was publishing cheap editions in small format for a public with little to spend upon books. But we owe him respect for having produced an engraving on wood of More which is authentic, if not elegant.

This cannot be said of another early woodcut. *La Prosopographie, ou description des personnes insignes* of Antoine du Verdier is an early example of the illustrated biographical compilations which were common towards the end of the sixteenth century. They are interesting because they are among the first publications designed for a literate but not scholarly public. The first edition of du Verdier's work came out in 1573 and it contained, above a short biography, a circular medallion with the legend THOMAS MORVS. If it is based on a miniature of More at all, it must have been painted before Holbein's likenesses, for the face is a young one, with hair down to the shoulders. It is possible that the block was later suppressed[1] as too poor a likeness, for it does not appear in subsequent editions of the *Prosopographie*.

These two woodcuts, however, are to some extent isolated from the three main groups into which subsequent portraits of More can be divided, which represent a considerable divergence from the Holbein image. It is perhaps a coincidence, but the first group to appear—which is also in some ways that which differs most from the Holbein image—is the first in which the relatively new medium of copper engraving is employed. Metal engraving as a medium of decoration had been a normal part of the goldsmith's craft from antiquity, but the adequate provision of the paper necessary for its commercial exploitation from engraved plates dates only from the fifteenth century. The art came to a high point of development in Italy with the work of Antonio Pollaiuolo (1432–98), the sculptor, goldsmith and painter of North Italy. The great exponents of the art in Northern Europe were Albrecht Dürer of Nuremberg (1471–1528) and Lucas van Leyden of Antwerp (1494–1533). In Antwerp, then the richest city in the world, artists and engravers congregated as nowhere else.

Lucas was also the first in the Netherlands to practise etching, a process by which a plate

---

[1] Or it may have been lost. It is difficult to say precisely when the block was removed, because (like many such compilations) individual copies of the *Prosopographie* vary in contents. It is certainly missing in the expanded edition of 1603.

is not engraved by a tool but bitten by acid. Towards 1521 he practised a unique fineness of line which gave a new stimulus to the art. In the hands of the next generation engraving became so subtle and versatile as to foreshadow the later development of the art known as mezzotint, principal among the exponents of which were the engraver-publishers of Antwerp.

THE GALLE VERSION

It was in Antwerp, in 1572, that Philip Galle published his *Virorum Doctorum . . . Effigies*, which contains a version of More's features that is totally independent of the Holbein painting or of Fowler's engraving. The hair hangs down and is not flicked back as in the miniatures, the chin is long, the lips slightly protuberant, the nose prominent and slightly irregular, but the nostrils are pinched and drawn back, not fleshy as Holbein painted them. In the Holbein versions the ear-pieces are attached to the cap or to a band beneath an outer cap. Galle shews earpieces continuous with the raised brim. There is a slight novelty in the arrangement of the furred robe, and beneath it More now wears a black semi-clerical vest with a single white frill visible at the neckline. This garment is a total departure from Holbein's furred neckline with a trace of white collar, but no frill visible above it. And, superficially, even more novel is the absence of the chain from which More refused to part even when he was led to the Tower, where he knew that, according to custom, it must be taken as a perquisite either of the king or, if he were lucky, of the lieutenant.

202:19

But are we to suppose that the only acceptable authority for a portrait of More was (or is) the original painting by Holbein; that is to say the portrait which, there is reason to believe, was no longer in London after 1535; or, on the other hand, the detail from one of the copies of the family portrait that was accessible; or, perhaps, the miniatures that were certainly in circulation? Because we are so habituated to the generalized portrait of More that derives from Holbein's painting, and hence expect to see the chain in every rendering, we are not entitled to assume that this painting or a copy of it must have been the only authority that an engraver would respect. To us a portrait of More without the chain does not 'look right', but we should be wrong to think that this was so to all his sixteenth-century admirers.[1] The two Windsor drawings, for instance, do not depict More wearing his chain.

The precedent set up by the painting, the miniatures and Fowler's woodcut makes it certain that Galle had before him none of these or their derivations. The omission of the chain by Galle may have been in the interest not only of novelty but of context, for his engraving appears in a volume intended to display celebrated doctors of learning, not officers of state—though it must be admitted that few publishers would view the matter scrupulously.

That Galle may have intended to portray the humanist as he was say in 1516, when he published *Utopia*, and before the chain was conferred, is not certain; for Galle does not give his subject a youthful appearance. No mention is made of More's age. While Galle

---

[1] All the same, in all the history of portrait engraving, engravers have shewn little reluctance to invent a portrait, when no authentic likeness was available.

reproduces Fowler's legend THOMAS MORVS ANGLVS he omits 'anno aetatis 50'. The priority of his publication and the excellence of his craftsmanship conferred upon his plate a precedence and quality that gave it wide currency on the Continent.

The first copy appears in another biographical collection like du Verdier's, which was put out in several different languages by the distinguished Lyon printer, Guillaume Rouillé. It too is a small woodcut medallion, and is a poor but recognizable adaptation of Galle. It does not appear, naturally enough, in the early editions published in the fifties and sixties, in which no biography of More appeared. The first impression is probably to be found in the second edition of the second part[1] in 1578.

A better—but anonymous—copy (in reverse) probably appeared about the same time. Only single prints are known, but it may have been part of a pirated version of Galle's collection, for incorporated on the plate (where in Galle they are printed separately) are not only the same inscription and four lines of verse celebrating More's learning, faith, bravery and piety, but also the same page signature. Although competently done, there is a mechanical quality in the copying, which indicates a degree of carelessness or haste. André Thevet's *Vies des Hommes Illustres* (Paris, 1584) also contains a copy, though freer in its treatment of detail. The amount of fur on the robe—a texture in which the other engravers revelled—was reduced to a barely recognizable fringe, and the right hand holds a quill instead of a scroll. The features are exaggerated to give a quite unfamiliar aspect of severity and austerity.

The last and best of the contemporary copies is that which appears in one of the most elaborate collections of portraits of the period. In 1597 Theodore de Bry (1528–98), a Fleming exiled for religion in 1570, began to publish his *Icones virorum illustrium*. The portraits were collected mainly by J. J. Boissard, who states in the preface that they were, as far as possible, *ad vivum*. But the model for the portrait of More, which appears in the second volume, is quite clearly Galle, though a number of interesting additions have been made. The plate has an elaborate arch, which carries the legend THOMAS MORUS CANCELLARIUS ANGLIAE. More carries a scroll and has before him a table, thereon a candle with snuffers, an open book and a tablet inscribed 'Nascitur Angliae, Obtruncatur 7 Jullii, Anno 1536' (sic; the last figure may have been altered from or to a '5'). The plate is signed with the monogram of R. Boissard, brother of the compiler. Though a piece of shop-work, it is of great importance because the book in which it appeared being small in format, relatively cheap, and therefore widely circulated, was often reprinted and frequently plagiarized, a not unnatural result of its favourable place of publication—Frankfurt was the great north-European centre of the bookselling trade. The last appearance of Galle's likeness is the frontispiece to the complete edition of More's Latin works, published, also at Frankfurt, by Christian Gensch in 1689.

[1] The Latin version is *Promptuarii iconum insigniorum a seculo hominum . . . pars secunda*. The cuts are generally attributed to Georges Réverdy.

4. THE INFLUENCE OF ANTON WIERICX'S VERSION

ANTWERP, however, retained its position as the artistically more significant centre of the graphic arts; and, in particular, of the crafts of engraving on copper. The artists employed by the Frankfurt publishers were decidedly inferior to the Netherlanders at this time, that is, towards the end of the sixteenth century and the beginning of the seventeenth. It is not surprising, therefore, that there should come from Antwerp at this time an engraved portrait, independent of Fowler or Galle, or of Boissard. Unfortunately it is very difficult to date, but it was certainly cut before 1624 and there may be solid reasons for dating it before, and well before, 1612. It was engraved on copper in Antwerp and is signed '*Anton Wierx fecit et excud*'.[1] He, like others of his family, was a prolific engraver. He was born in 1552 and is not heard of after 1624. It is an important plate.

210:21

At first glance, the composition of this plate resembles that of Fowler's wood-block, and thus, cursorily, might be related to a 'Holbein' model. The costume, the set of the subject and the chain (although plain and without the SS), recall such a model. However, the plate is oblong, and without the border and inscription measures $2\frac{9}{16} \times 3\frac{9}{16}$ in. The inscription, set out on a tablet $\frac{3}{8}$ in. in depth reads: 'THOMAS MORVS QVONDAM SVPREMVS TOTIVS ANGLIAE CANCELLARIVS DIGNISS', a form of words that will need comment. The portrait itself, however, does not convey the same impression as the miniatures with which we are familar. Wiericx gives More an expression of anxiety in the place of the serenity that Holbein conveys. But there is no reason to doubt that the engraver took trouble, so far as he could, to acquire an authentic model.

Wiericx was an engraver only of monarchs, dukes and of truly famous and eminent men. His portraits, say of Rudolph II, the contemporary head of the Holy Roman Empire, of Philip, Duke of Lorraine and William, Count Palatine are superb specimens of engraving in the subtle style. It is disagreeable to be obliged to report that the same artist's plate of More is not of equal merit. It is by no means a poor piece of work though not of Anton Wiericx at his best. It is clear that he was attempting a portrait not merely of the author of *Utopia*, but of the former most worthy chancellor of England who had fallen from that high dignity. The keyword of the inscription is 'quondam'. It would be rash to say positively that Wiericx was the first to employ the word 'quondam' in a description engraved on a plate of More. That appears to be the fact. The word 'engraved' is emphasized because there is a painted description in the same terms that we shall have to examine in due time, but for the moment let us disregard the question of any earlier appearance of the description.

[1] Another state is also known (in the print room of the Royal Library, Brussels) signed '*Anton Wierx fecit Hieronymus Wirx excud*'.

51

The immediate point to remember is that the form used by Fowler in 1568 was THOMAS MORVS ANGLVS ANNO AETATIS 50 and that of de Bry in 1598 was THOMAS MORUS CANCELLARIUS ANGLIAE. Leaving aside the verses or couplets that were part of the convention in the larger prints of the period, it will be recognized that the title QVONDAM SVPREMVS TOTIVS ANGLIAE CANCELLARIVS DIGNISS. marks an increase in the estimate accorded to the worldly eminence of More in the mind, at least, of the publishing, bookselling and print-selling trade. We shall have to return to the question of Wiericx's authority for this text, as also of the portrait itself. Meanwhile it is necessary to attend the awkward question left by this engraver's habit of not dating his work and that the historians of engraving in the Netherlands, such as Alvin and Rooses and Wurzbach, have not been able to say more than that Anton Wiericx is not heard of after 1624. As a precocious artist he began work at the age of 14 and may have turned to religious portraiture when the Antwerp Jesuits, following the precept of Ignatius and the example of Canisius, procured the publication of superbly illustrated catechetical and devotional works, many of whose plates came from the hands of the Wiericx family. Anton is represented, with his two brothers, in the finest of all such publications, the *Evangelicae Historiae Imagines* of Jerónimo Nadal, S.J. (*Latine* Hieronymus Natalis). It is necessary to say something about this book—not because it directly concerns More but because it incidentally concerns the date of Wiericx's portrait.

This is the most ambitious and impressive of all the illustrated books of instruction and devotion that the Jesuits (or anybody else) contrived in the interest of the Counter-Reformation. It was aimed at the rich and cultivated bourgeoisie, not only of Antwerp, and is worthy of that target. A folio, it consists of no fewer than 153 engravings upon which the three Wiericx brothers worked. It would take us too far to recount the history of this magnificent book. But it will not be a digression to explain that the altogether extraordinarily high quality of the work is due to a significant fact. Father Nadal was the greatest of all the early Jesuits after Ignatius Loyola. He was a Spaniard from Palma in Majorca and though he knew Ignatius in his Paris University days, and was intimate with him, it was not until Nadal met Francis Xavier that he offered himself to the new group. According to Father Brodrick, S.J., Nadal became the second founder of the Society. There is, indeed, much to be said about this extraordinary man. However, to stick to the point, among other promises Nadal made to Ignatius, was one to write a commentary on the Epistles and Gospels as they are read at Mass, illustrate them with pictures and to comment thereupon. This was finally accomplished. The text occupies 650 pages, mainly set in double column, the whole of folio size, equally with the illustrations. This, roughly, was the conception of Ignatius Loyola and Jerónimo Nadal. Ignatius died in 1556; Nadal in 1580. The burden of executing the wish of the founder fell upon two Spaniards of the Roman college of the Society, and it was Diego and Emmanuel Ximenez who brought the book to its perfection— and it is nothing less. Diego was the faithful companion of Nadal in all his missionary journeys. The Jesuits had worked on it for forty years. Their plan required the collaboration of the finest available artists and printers. The originals are the work mainly of Bernardo

Figure 19. Engraving by Philip Galle, 1572 (202)

Figure 20. Engraving by R. Boissard, 1598 (209)

THOMAS MORUS CANCELLARIUS ANGLIÆ.

Nascitur Anglia,
Obtruncatur 7ᵉ
Iulij Anno 1535.

Singultantem animam Morj, taboque natantem
Abluit hej Pietas ipsa suis lachrimis.

Figure 21. Engraving by Anton Wiericx, *ante* 1612 (210)

Figure 22. Engraving by J. Faber, 1612 (212)

Figure 23. Engraving, probably by Willem or Magdalena van de Passe, 1620 (213)

Disce Mori Mundo:
Iiuere Disce Deo.

UERA EFFIGIES THOMÆ MORI QUONDAM TOTIUS ANGLIÆ CANCELLARII DIGNISSIMI · ETc d

The true Portraicture of S THOMAS MORE. some:
tymes Lord Chanceloure of England. famous for letters.
He died Anno 1 5 3 4.

Are to be sold by Compton Holland ouer against the Exchange.   R: Elstracke sculp:

Figure 24. Engraving by Renold Elstracke, c. 1620 (214)

Figures 25 and 26. Silver medallion, probably by Simon van de Passe,
c. 1620, obverse and reverse (302)

Figure 27. Engraving by Valdor, 1621 (215)

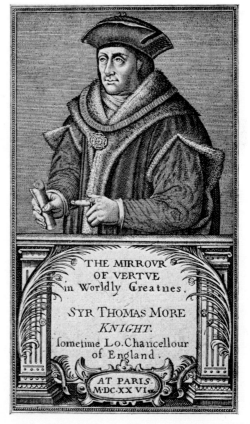

Figure 28. Engraved title to Roper's *Life of
More*, 1626 (216)

Figure 29. The miniature related to the Wiericx
engraving (104)

Figure 30. Woodcut by Tobias Stimmer, *c.* 1577 (204)

Figure 31. Engraving in Thomas Stapleton's *Tres
Thomae*, 1588 (208)

Pessaro of Rome and Martin de Vos of Antwerp. Anton, Jerome and Jean Wiericx, all three brothers, were occupied for six years on the task of engraving. The result, published in 1593, is superb. The point for us is that it shews Anton Wiericx at the height of his powers. He engraved fifty-eight of the hundred and sixty plates.

The relatively inferior quality of his More may be due to its having been accomplished before 1586 when Plantin, in behalf of the Roman Jesuits, reached agreement with 'les dicts Wiericx' and possibly even earlier still. Indeed, it is not impossible that Anton Wiericx could have cut the More plate soon after he was 21 and admitted to the Guild. This would have been in 1563, the year of the publication in Basel of the first collected edition of More's Latin works; which cannot but have stimulated soon afterwards a sale for his portrait in a size that would fit its small format.

But it can as well be argued that after his six years' hard labour from 1586 onwards in Nadal's book, Anton Wiericx would not be averse from exploiting his now great reputation by engraving the portraits of the territorial and literary aristocracy and therefore that the series of small plates signed by him date say from 1593 to 1603. If this were so it would account for the fact that no imitation of his plate appears to have been made in the sixteenth century and that when Frankfurt is found copying an engraving of More in 1598 it is Philip Galle's plate of 1572 that was exploited. Altogether, therefore, we may conclude that Anton Wiericx' plate was cut after 1598.

There is one, more positive, datum that helps the question: the German translation of *Utopia* that appeared at Leipzig in 1612. It is an ugly product of the publisher Henning Grossen. Among the preliminaries is a badly engraved copper plate of More. He wears the same expression as in the Wiericx plate, and the portrait is set above the same 'quondam' inscription. The engraver, Johann Faber junior, signs the composition and puts it in a crude baroque frame. As it is clearly not the product of any creative talent—Faber was employed by Henning Grossen to engrave maps and other odd jobs—it is reasonable to suppose that the Wiericx plate was the original; and, therefore, to fix the latter's date as before 1612.[1]
212:*22*

The date is the more important in view of the next development in the portraiture of More that calls for notice. That the Wiericx plate was known and in circulation among the book trade, and hence accessible to Henning Grossen as well as others, is confirmed by a later version, to be seen in the volume of contemporary portraits with text written by the London publisher, Henry Holland.
213:*23*

The title of the book is *Herω-ologia Anglica hoc est Clarissimorum et doctissimorum aliquot Anglorum qui floruerunt ab anno Cristi M.D. usque ad presentem annum MDCXX Vivae Effigies et elogia Duobus Tomis.* It is the sequel to the same editor's *Baziliωlogia*, a set of engravings of the English monarchs published two years earlier. Both books are fully described by

---

[1] In fact, the *terminus ante quem* may be put back a year more, to 1611, because in that year appeared V. Andreas's *Imagines Doctorum Virorum* which contains a minute and even rougher, but still recognizable, woodcut which is clearly influenced by Wiericx. It also shows some affinity with the engraving in *Tres Thomae*, so it may be derived from an independent miniature.
211

Hind;[1] they were printed in Arnhem from plates engraved by fine Dutch and other masters; as the sub-title of *Herω-ologia* has it, *Impensis Crispini Passaei &c.*

The acknowledged model of Holland's *Herω-ologia* was Jacob Verheiden's *Praestantium aliquot Theologorum qui Romanum Antichristum praecipue oppugnarent Effigies et Elogia* which was published at The Hague in 1602 with plates engraved by Hendrik Hondius. The purpose of the publication is made obvious in the title and Holland's intentions, expressed in the text he wrote for the book, were similar: to smite the Papists and exalt the Reformers. He thought fit to include More, who had been too much for Verheiden—he went no further than Erasmus. As to his originals, Holland claims that they were carefully verified. So far as possible, he had striven to get his subjects 'ut ab ipsis vivis imaginibus oleo depictis effingeretur'. The name of the artist responsible for making the drawings from the contemporary oil-paintings to which Holland resorted is not known. The engravings were evidently supervised by the famous Utrecht artist who, in fact, was in partnership with Holland. Crispin van de Passe the Elder (1564–1637) was one of the finest engravers of the age. He was famous in England for his portraits of Queen Elizabeth. The majority of the sixty-seven plates were (it is implied in the commendatory verses at the beginning) executed by two of Crispin's talented children, Willem and Magdalena van de Passe.

What credence can be given to Holland's claim that for the originals of his engravings he had sought out contemporary paintings? The only evidence, as far as his version of More is concerned, is to be found in the annotations of source which are found in a number of copies of the *Herω-ologia*. These are derived from an original which cannot certainly be traced back further than the late seventeenth century, but their value is still a matter of controversy.[2] Against the More is written 'At Richmond—Holbens', and this reference, whether authentic or not, is at present incapable of elucidation. None of the known versions of any of Holbein's delineations of More can certainly be said to have been at Richmond at the beginning of the seventeenth century. Yet, vague though it is, this scrap of evidence does something to support Holland's claim; which is welcome.

Otherwise it would be difficult to resist the conclusion that the model in this case was the Wiericx engraving which it so much resembles. As has been seen above, the Wiericx plate may have been engraved as early as 1591 but could not have been cut later than 1612, i.e. eight years before Van de Passe cut his plate in Holland's book. Both plates are Holbeinesque in sitting and costume, including the chain, however different they may be in countenance. Thus it is possible to argue that the Wiericx and the Van de Passe engravings depend, albeit at some distance, upon the Holbein painting and not, as Philip Galle's engraving does, upon a version unconnected with Holbein. Moreover, apart from AB's couplet 'Hic est ille Thomas', etc. the inscription in Van de Passe's plate is identical with that in Wiericx's: THOMAS MORVS QVONDAM SVPREMVS TOTIVS ANGLIAE, etc. The significant difference between the two is that the head in the Wiericx plate is of the customary round shape, whereas in the Van de Passe plate the head is relatively longer and the expression

---

[1] A. M. Hind, *Engraving in England in the 16th and 17th Centuries*, vol. II (1955), passim.
[2] See A. M. Hind, op. cit. vol. II, passim, pp. 151ff.

of the face more anxious. These features are even more marked in a fine enlarged copy, an 217
etching, of about the middle of the century, which shews the figure only without border or
background; the face, in particular, is given an almost sculptural intensity.

There is one other important consideration that needs to be borne in mind before it is
concluded that Holland's original was the Wiericx plate and not an oil painting. At the
Versailles museum there is a portrait in oils which is undoubtedly that of More. He is 26
costumed as in Holland's plate and the head is long rather than round in shape, as in that of
Wiericx. Obviously, the painting and the engraving are similar; obviously, too, they are
of the same period. The painting, however, has not been the subject of expert study. It is
not mentioned in any of the great works on seventeenth-century portraiture. It is not a
painting of great merit. Nothing is known of its origin. The Versailles gallery goes no further
than to say that this portrait of More is a 'peinture du XVIIme siècle' and that it was
formerly in the Sorbonne collection. The even more perfunctory rendering of the chain,
and the reduction of the rose to a formalized jewel, suggest that the painter was dependent
on the *Herω-ologia* engraving, and that he failed to grasp the significance of the detail.

More immediately connected with the Van de Passe plate is a small silver medallion of 302:25-6
which, like the bronze medallion described above, a unique example is in the British
Museum. It closely resembles the fine oval medallions of James I and other notables of the
early seventeenth century, engraved by Simon van de Passe, a third child of Crispin. The
medallion of More, though smaller and circular, is clearly by the same hand, and equally
clearly copied from the copper plate in the *Herω-ologia*. The reverse shows St Thomas of
Canterbury, a pairing suggested no doubt by Stapleton's *Tres Thomae*, published in 1588.
This, and the inscription on the obverse, the first datable explicit description of More as
'martyr', must indicate that it was designed for Catholic use, and it is curious that members
of the same family should have been busy with the Protestant *Herω-ologia* at the same time.[1]

Another plate obviously indebted to Wiericx needs to be recorded. Apparently, the only 218
print is in the Bibliothèque Nationale, but it would, of course, be rash to argue that the
engraver was a Parisian. The descriptive legend corresponds with that of Wiericx, except
that the inscription omits the final word DIGNISS. From appearances the plate could be
dated perhaps as early as 1620 and not later than 1640. The signature, 'Cd', is unknown to
Bénézit, nor are any other specimens of his work recorded. In any case 'Cd' must be ranked
with the many humble workers for the publishers of the period. Its only importance is that
it witnesses to the continuing influence of Wiericx.

In chronological order, so far as it can be determined, the next is an independent plate,
which also exercised a distinct influence upon later engravers. The new plate is dedicated 215:27
to Christopher de Blocquerie, archdeacon of Liège, by the engraver, Jean Valdor (1590–
1661), to whom we are the more grateful since he chose to date it. He engraved his portrait
of More in 1621. The legend reads: EFFIGIES THOMAE MORI Supremi quondam Angliae
Cancellarii *Quam ad vivum expressam*. There is a liveliness in this version which is fresh even

---

[1] But engravers rarely jibbed at working for both sides, if both were prepared to pay.

if the first impulse should derive from Wiericx. The expression on More's face is changed. He is now cheerful, his cheeks ample, there is no loss of dignity, and his presence has greater assurance.[1] Valdor's version is three-quarter length. More's right hand, wearing a signet-ring, points to a scroll grasped in his left. These elements are also present in a plate engraved at almost the same time, perhaps slightly earlier, by a Flemish engraver formerly associated with Crispin van de Passe, who later worked in London. This plate was to prove as influential as a source for copying in England as the two former in France, until the end of the century.

Among the engravers practising in England at the turn of the sixteenth century was Renold Elstracke (*floruit* 1598–1625). He worked for many years in conjunction with the printsellers, Henry Holland and Compton Holland, for whom he engraved numerous **214:24** portraits, maps, title-pages, and a mass of other subjects. No. 53 is the plate of More. The portrait is set within an oval frame, surrounded by coats-of-arms and other ornaments. The inscription in the oval border reads UERA EFFIGIES THOMAE MORI QVONDAM TOTIUS ANGLIAE CANCELLARII DIGNISSIMI. ETc. Below the portrait is an entablature in which the following text appears:

The true Portraicture of Sʳ THOMAS MORE. some: tymes Lord Chanceloure of England. famous for letters. He died Anno 1534. Are to be sold by Compton Holland ouer against the Exchange. R: Elstracke sculp:

The Lord Chancellor is in his robes but Elstracke, like Valdor, alters the lower portion of the figure by placing a scroll in his right hand and the great seal in his left. Also, Elstracke includes a table upon which he rests his left arm. An additional piece of furniture is the great purse. The plate therefore is notably independent of Van de Passe's cut in Holland's *Herω-ologia* of 1620. However, the ornamental style of the portrait, arranged in an oval, with decorations in the spandrels and providing a text at foot, was originated for Holland's *Baziliωlogia* of 1618, upon which Elstracke worked. What then is the date of Elstracke's plate? Nothing is known of the engraver after 1625.

According to the custom of the trade in Antwerp and elsewhere, prints were sold separately at the time of their engraving, which in many instances would have been well before their collection with others and publication in book form. As the market for portraits was then so profitable many hands co-operated in the production of sets in book-form. Hence, these sets or albums comprise the work of several artists, even though one engraver-publisher would take the risk. In some instances the engraver himself made first a drawing of the portrait, but not in all instances.

As to Elstracke's More, all we know is that he was responsible for the engraving. If Compton Holland had collected his portraits into a volume, it might have thrown light upon the date and location of a similar painting, since lost. It is the more disappointing that Elstracke's print cannot be dated with any precision, since the design was copied in varying degrees of faithfulness until the time of Thomas Hearne, as will be duly reported. The

---

[1] It is possible, however, that this change does not represent the actual intention of the engraver, but is the purely mechanical result of inaccurate 'squaring' in the process of transferring the original, whether Wiericx's engraving or not, on to a new copper plate.

Hollands appear to have died or retired from publishing about 1621. The vagueness of this date is again unfortunate. All we can say is that Elstracke's plate was produced by about 1621. But this is not a negligible *terminus ad quem*, for it permits us to place it in correct relation with the very interesting engraving that appears next in chronological order as far as it can be established. But it is not possible to say whether, as seems likely, it anticipated Valdor's plate which is definitely dated by him as 1621. The plate itself survived for some considerable time and is found, with Compton Holland's name beaten out and that of 'John Hind' substituted for it, as the frontispiece to Cresacre More's *Life and Death of Sᵣ Thomas More* (1642). Ten years later it appears again with all below the frame cut away, in John Hoddesdon's *Tho: Mori Vita et Exitus*.[1] It became in fact the model for the seventeenth century as Galle's had been in the sixteenth. It probably served thus for two minute portraits—although one of them has a beard—for two popular books of proverbs and saws.[2] Finally, it left its mark on the engravings of the turn of the century when the Holbein image became known again. But if it is possible that Valdor's plate was copied from Elstracke, it is certain that Valdor's plate was the model for another engraving which appeared five years later.

222–3

In 1626 occurred an event capital in the historiography of More. Thomas Stapleton's *Vita Mori* had remained in Latin since 1588. During the intervening period, Roper's account of More was still in manuscript. It had probably been accessible to Stapleton. The manuscript was written *c.* 1555 and was still on the shelf when its author died in 1578. It was a year that witnessed an event of importance to the English Catholics, the new generation of which, that had grown up since 1559, was determined not to give up the old Mass and not attend the new services. But the conditions in England in which the resistance worked were not easier. Also, the situation in Flanders, the centre of Catholic propagandist activity, was more difficult. The Spanish regime, despite its power, was less secure.

In 1578 the magistrates of Douai, who strongly favoured the Prince of Orange, ordered the English refugees out and Allen thereupon removed the college to Rheims. About the same time the Jesuits decided to engage upon their dangerous mission to England. Whether Roper's executors intended his manuscript to be printed secretly in England, but kept it back when the Jesuit press in England was discovered in 1581, cannot be known. But certainly the book was much copied and widely circulated in manuscript. Naturally, in due course it found its way to the Jesuits. After much delay, they put it to press 'at Paris', i.e. from Saint Omer, the college established by Father Persons, S.J. in 1592. Thus the first edition of Roper's book, THE MIRROVR OF VERTVE in Wordly Greatnes *Syr Thomas More, Knight*, was printed at their foreign press in 1626. Its engraved title-page includes a portrait of More which resembles the Valdor plate of 1621. The figure is three-quarter length, faces to the left, holds a scroll and wears a signet ring. There are slight differences and numerous deficiencies that indicate a less able hand. The features in the Jesuit version are

216:28

---

[1] It is even sometimes found, similarly cut down and with the plate even more worn, as late as the 1724 edition of Erasmus's *Moriae Encomium*.

[2] Cotgrave's *Wits Interpreter* (1655) and Bayley's *Witty Apophthegmes* (1658).

plumper and the expression more benign, but the mouth is weaker. Nevertheless, the rendering was appreciated by its public and accorded a considerable measure of authority or, at least, approval.

A variant of it is to be found inserted perhaps by the contemporary owner as a frontispiece of one of the many manuscript copies of Roper's *Life* made during the persecution. One among these, B.M. Ms. Harley 6254, contains a portrait based on the Wiericx-Valdor-Saint Omer tradition. The figure is holding the scroll and wears his signet ring, thus shewing the influence of Elstracke. The text, set in an arch, varies from precedent and ascends to a panegyric: THOMAS MORVS QVONDAM ANGLIAE CANCELLARIVS SVI SAECVLI DELICIVM ET ERVDITIONIS DECVS. The date of the print in Harley 6254 may be taken as between 1620 and 1640. The engraving itself is a mediocre piece of work, performed perhaps in England. That it was embodied in Harley 6254 may be significant; a print on vellum was lent by the Carmelite Convent at Darlington to the More Memorial Exhibition at Chelsea in 1929. It was copied by Michael Burgers, *c.* 1714, at the request of Hearne, who has the MS. on loan from John Murray, the London bookseller.

However, when William Marshall engraved the plate which provided the title page for editions both of More's *Epigrams* (1638) and *Utopia* (1639), he reverted to the *Herω-ologia* likeness, and it lasted on till the end of the century, a poor (and curiously savage-looking) copy being annexed to Paul Freher's *Theatrum Virorum Eruditione Clarorum* (Nürnberg, 1688). Its last appearance is in Isaac de Larrey's *Histoire d'Angleterre* (Rotterdam, 1697–8), for which it was copied by Adrian van de Werft and engraved by Peter Stevens van Gunst, in a grandiose baroque frame.[1]

In fact it is to be seen that it is not easy to identify the authority that lies behind any one of the engraved portraits. Certainly the medal and the miniature created a market for a cheaper medium, the engraved print on vellum or paper. Such a medium, printed in plain black ink and capable of wide distribution, was also capable of arousing admiration when dignified by being coloured. There exist in the British Museum several prints of the portrait of Saint Ignatius Loyola engraved by Anton Wiericx in the same format as his More. One of these is superbly tinctured in scarlet, ultramarine and green, and illuminated in gold. From it a good painter could have made a handsome altar piece. When, therefore, a miniature painting and an engraved print closely resemble each other, it is hard to determine which of the two is the model—unless there is a contemporary document to confirm the priority. Is there then any representation of More not mentioned by the art historians which may have served as the basis for other portraits and miniatures and the engraving by Wiericx?

That the scroll, signet ring and purse appear in the later (i.e. those of Valdor and Elstracke) engravings gives rise to the question whether there may lie behind these, too, a painting which has been their pattern or has contributed to it. It is true that the scroll and the ring appear in the New York portrait in simple form; but Valdor and Elstracke dramatize

220

233

228

231

___

[1] Though this in turn, it appears, was copied for a biographical dictionary in England towards the end of the eighteenth century.

them. Hence, what these plates do is to foreshadow the conventions of pictorial journalism of the present day; and, therefore, it is not necessary to assume that the authority for some of them, e.g. of Valdor and Elstracke, is an oil painting or a miniature of which no trace remains. The scroll, the ring and the purse and other additions in the way of furniture do not by themselves prove the existence of another authoritative portrait of the man.

Thus we approach this question: since a connection, direct or indirect, with a miniature almost certainly occurs in John Fowler's oval woodcut of 1563, can a similar degree of coincidence be pointed to in any other instance? Not, it must be admitted, in the case of Philip Galle whose plate is one of the models for other engravers of the last quarter of the sixteenth century. What of the next century? Is there a painting whose authority lay behind the most influential of the prints of the early seventeenth century? What lies behind the plate of Anton Wiericx, the first engraver to employ the word 'quondam' which became standard in so many later inscriptions on engraved plates of More?

There is a miniature painting whose relevance has not been appreciated since it was first recorded and reproduced more than forty years ago in the *Catalogue of the Library of Charles Fairfax Murray*. The catalogue was compiled by the late H. W. Davies, a bibliographer of rare learning, particularly in engraved portraiture. It was published in two volumes in 1913, in an edition of one hundred copies. Mr Davies, having described the edition, proceeded to say of the miniature that it was probably the original of the (reversed) engraving by Jan Faber, Junior, in the German translation of *Utopia* (Leipzig, 1612). This very valuable observation was overlooked at the time it was made. The war of 1914–18 had, of course, the incidental effect of postponing all bibliographical effort and of preventing any attention being given to Mr Davies's book, and the entry, accompanied as it was by a facsimile, remained unknown, like the original to which it referred. It is well to emphasize the fact that the mention in 1913 is the first in literature.

The miniature itself occurs in an improbable position—inserted before the initial page of the text of the first collected edition of More's Latin works, printed under the title of *Lucubrationes* (Basel, 1563). It is not a circle like the other three miniatures, intended for preservation or display in a locket but an upright rectangle painted upon a sheet of vellum cut to the size of the book. Though the grey hair flicked back recalls the Lincoln's Inn miniature, there are notable differences. The nose is high bridged, the chain is a continuous cable, with no indication of the SS original constituents and no portcullis clasps. That the likeness was achieved after More's fall is proved by the inscription which reads THOMAS MORVS QVONDĀ SUPREM⁹ TOTI⁹ ANGLIAE CANCELLARI⁹ DIGN.

The contraction '9' for US in this legend may provide some guide to the origin of the miniature. It is, in fact, a German convention current up to the end of the seventeenth century; it may be seen in an inscription in the Cathedral of Mainz which is dated 1558.[1] For what a guess is worth it may be conjectured that this miniature is the work of a German artist employed by a bookseller, perhaps in Basel. Furthermore it may be safely said that if it is not the source behind Wiericx, just as he is the source behind Faber, it is derived from

[1] F. V. Arens and K. F. Bauer, *Die deutschen Inschriften*, vol. II, 3, no. 444.

the same source as Wiericx. In other words, Wiericx is dependent upon this miniature or one closely similar in size, shape and expression. The further possibility must not be dismissed that it was copied from Wiericx's engraving.

The Fairfax Murray collection of German books, including the edition of More containing the miniature, was sold at Christies in December 1917. The description of lot No. 315 was calculated to arouse interest. The copy of the *Lucubrationes* was special, as being garnished 'with a painted miniature portrait of More on vellum, inserted as a frontispiece'. A supplementary note drew attention to 'the fine miniature of More, in gold and brilliant colours [which] represents him in hat, fur-trimmed robes and gold chain, with Tudor rose'. Without further publicity, the volume with miniature was acquired by John Burns, well known as a collector of More's works in all editions and languages. After he died in 1943 his books were sold at Sotheby's. The volume again came up. In the catalogue, as lot No. 7, it was described laconically as an edition of the *Lucubrationes* of 1563 'with a miniature of More inserted'. It did not receive special notice and reached the sum of £32 in February 1944. We must now try to deal with its date.

The oblong form is not common early in the sixteenth century. Horenbout, the king's chief limner, executed a rectangular ($2 \times 1\frac{3}{4}$ in.) miniature of Henry VIII before 1544, but the form is not again found until Isaac Oliver's Portrait of a Young Man was painted, not earlier than 1590. The scale then is larger, $5 \times 3\frac{1}{2}$ in. The normal alternative to the circular was the oval form, which was favoured by Hilliard and the artist who painted the original that Fowler gave to his wood-engraver. It seems, therefore, that the rectangle or oblong is a later development. Whereas the oval naturally springs from the circle, the rectangle hardly does. Moreover, the purpose of a rectangular miniature cannot be to fit a circular or oval locket. What would be the purpose of an upright rectangle of the size of the miniature now under discussion? Clearly, it must have been to bind or paste it into a book—a custom that became prevalent in the second half of the sixteenth century, when a bookseller would provide a portrait of the author for insertion in the purchased edition of his book.

The first collected edition of More's Latin works is a practical, pocketable edition and must greatly have spread More's fame all over the Continent. We may reasonably expect miniatures, whether painted or printed, circular or rectangular, soon after that date. Sure enough, the woodcuts and engravings follow within a few years. To sum up then, we have here a miniature so closely related to the Wiericx engraving that we may say with some safety that the one must be copied from the other. The arguments for a German or Swiss origin seem convincing. On the other hand it is not impossible to connect it, at several removes, with the work of the mid-sixteenth century limners, who at best could produce first-class miniatures, and at worst the hack figures for initials on official documents; the latter would be common enough anywhere in Europe.

Figure 32. The version by Rubens (8)

THOMAS MORIS

Et uerae iunxit religionis amor.
Ob quem carnificis uos perculit una securis.
Vná que nex binis, unaque causa necis.
Quàm bene caelesti iunctorum sede duorum
Iunxit et effigies una tabella duas!

Figure 33. Engraving by Frans van de Wungaerde, *c.* 1650 (224)

Figures 34 and 35. Engraved frontispiece and title-page to Regi, *Vita di Tomaso Moro*, 1675 (226)

Figure 36. Engraving by G. Vertue, 1726 (235)

Figure 37. Engraving by R. White, 1679 (227)

5. OTHER VERSIONS OF ABOUT 1600

BEFORE passing on to the third, later, group of engravings, it may be expedient to consider the isolated representations which do not fit into any of the groups mentioned. First of all there is a woodcut by Tobias Stimmer, a lively and effective delinea- 204:30 tion, but not a good likeness. The fact that it was first produced at Basel encourages the supposition that it might be based on the family group drawing, then in the possession of the Amerbach family. There is, however, no resemblance, and it is difficult to see what it derives from, unless it were a very poor copy of the type of miniature from which Fowler's cut was taken. Stimmer's appears for the first time, well impressed, in a late edition of the prolific Paolo Giovio's *Elogia Virorum Litteris Illustrium* (Basel, 1577); it is noticeable that its border is already broken at the top, slightly to the left. The same block, with the same break, appears in Theodor Zwinger's *Icones Aliquot Clarorum Virorum*, which was printed—also in Basel—as an appendix to Nicolaus Reusner's *Icones sive Imagines vivae* (1589). It may be found yet a third time, the break still recognizable, as late as 1690, in Johann Gottfried Zeidler's *Theatri Eruditorum . . . Compendium*, by which time it had moved to Wittenberg.

The engraving which appears in Thomas Stapleton's *Tres Thomae* (Douai 1588) ought to 208:31 be an important one. Stapleton's careful description of More has already been quoted, but it is clear that he was unable to amplify his words with a portrait by a first-rate craftsman. Nevertheless, although it suffers from the lifelessness which afflicts the work of the inferior artist, the engraving has some points which indicate that a good deal of care was devoted to it. For instance, the eyes are well-set, and, with the nose, have a faint resemblance to the Holbein image. More noticeable, the chain of SS is accurately rendered (except for the clasp), uniquely so among the early engravings. The cap is peculiar to this likeness; the right hand is pointed in the direction of the paper held in the left, but not actually *at* it, as in the Elstracke-Valdor prints. The face, too, is full, without the hollows of the Wiericx-Van de Passe or Galle versions. While it can hardly be the direct original of the Elstracke-Valdor prints, there may have been an original common to both, which, if it belonged to any of the members of More's household then at Douai, would have a very high degree of authenticity.

A third portrait which may be briefly mentioned is a painting at Badminton. It is a poor 27 likeness, compared with any of the others, but it has a vestigial interest because in some respects it appears to combine certain features of the 'non-Holbein' images with others which are found in the Frick type of portrait. The features are harsh and there is no chain, but the cap and the smaller dark eyes suggest Holbein. It may, however, be only a late conflation of already existing and divergent elements, in which case it cannot be a link of this sort.

Another interesting version, also no strong likeness, is the canvas in the collection of the Earl of Leicester at Holkham Hall. It is in fact not easily recognizable as More, and the flat cap he is shewn wearing is unlike those shewn in any other portrait. The inscription at the top, however, D. THOMAS MORUS MAGNUS ANGLIAE CANCELL . . . . . SUB HENR. VIII MARTYR., is the first painted version in which he is so described. It well accords with this wording that Spain may be conjectured to be the place of origin of this picture. The basis for this is the superscription on the letter which he holds in his left hand, which reads: *Al Illmo Tomas M* . . . . It would be interesting to connect this painting with the last and most interesting of these early free renderings, but it is unlikely that this latter picture, which was in Antwerp in 1652, could have reached Spain before the Holkham portrait was painted; there is, moreover, no obvious resemblance between the two.

We come then, to the last of the independent versions, whose importance merits separate consideration.

There is in the Prado in Madrid a portrait by Rubens on the grand scale, based on one of the versions of Holbein's single portrait. It is a fairly free copy, showing more of the body, and omitting the collar of SS; it seems to indicate the curl on the left temple. Its date is uncertain. Traditionally, it has been held to be a late production, Max Rooses suggesting 1630–35, and others 1629–30 (apparently on the assumption that it was painted during Rubens's visit to England then). Stylistically, 1615–20 seems a more probable guess. No Rubens scholar has recently considered the dating, and no one has put forward the suggestion that it was painted in Italy, before Rubens's return to Flanders in 1609, which, if it could be established, would provide a shred of confirmation to the early, semi-fabulous, history of the Frick version.

According to the Prado catalogues, the painting was acquired for Isabella Farnese; it may be presumed to be the same as

een schildereye oock geschildert door denselven Rubens, wesende het contrefeytsel van Thomas Morus[1]

recorded in the inventory of Jan van Meurs at Antwerp in 1652. If this is so, it could have been based on the Orleans version, which, it will be remembered, was also in Antwerp at this time, and might have been there earlier.[2]

Did Rubens see the Frick version in Rome? Or did he paint it towards the end of his life, back at Antwerp? Is it possible that he worked from a copy of one of Holbein's preparatory sketches? We cannot say. But, as in the Windsor drawings, the chain is omitted; also the features are, similarly, more youthful. No reproductions are to be found that derive directly or indirectly from the Rubens original.[3] We should have been fortunate had the Rubens portrait been engraved by a Theodore de Galle or a Charles de Mallery. It was the earlier tradition deriving from Antwerp that continued to dominate the school of engraving.[4]

[1] J. Denucé, *The Antwerp Art Galleries*, p. 135.   [2] See p. 12.
[3] Except for a remarkably bad lithograph by Sensi done in 1858.
[4] One further seventeenth-century painting may be mentioned. According to an article in *The Times*, 23 May 1961, p. 15, *The Learned Art of Mattia Preti*, the baroque artist Preti, famous for his church decorations in Malta, executed a picture of More in prison.

6. LATER ENGRAVINGS: A THIRD VERSION?

THE third group consists entirely of engravings; these present a number of problems which cannot be said to have been solved. A possible line of connection will be put forward, but it must be emphasized that it is based on highly conjectural grounds.

The starting point may be taken to be the fine, if atypical, undated engraving by Frans 224:*33* van den Wyngaerde of Antwerp (1614–79). Regrettably little is known of this able engraver. He practised a fine line in plates of large rectangular scale which gives his subjects power as well as grace. He engraved relatively few plates, but all are excellent. His More follows, in outline, the Holbein portrait; however, it makes use of a certain freedom in the choice and representation of details, but without compromising the likeness. The head faces to the left, whereas in the Holbein originals the face is towards the right. This change of direction is, of course, of no significance in an engraving. More's hair is brushed back on the right side, the nose a compromise between the fleshy, powerful, shape painted in the New York portrait and the straighter version adopted in the miniatures. The robe is arranged differently as to the sleeve on the spectator's left, and folds over in front, leaving visible a black undervest. The fur on the neck of the robe is cut with care and shown as ermine, not sable. It seems certain that Wyngaerde had, in More's case, access to a painting as his authority, for he includes the chain. This does not appear in Galle's plate of 1572 or in either of the Windsor drawings, and, though it does in the miniatures and in the Wiericx engraving, Wyngaerde's treatment of it is so different as to preclude the possibility of imitation. It is possible that Wyngaerde took as his immediate model a good version of the double portraits of More Cf. 51 and Fisher based on Holbein, of which later copies exist. As he did not understand the significance of the SS, he engraved a twin-cabled, rope-like ornament which terminates in two hands that clasp a ring from which the rose is suspended.

Beneath are five lines, indifferently cut by a local hack, though themselves an admirable composition. The final lines read:

> Quam bene caelesti junctorum sede duorum
> Iunxit et effigies una tabella duas.

The explanation is that the picture is one of a pair engraved on the same double plate, the other being of John Fisher. The engraving of More exists in more than one state, the earlier (one assumes) being that without the frame or the attribution to Holbein. It is unfortunate that the date of Wyngaerde's engraving has not been found, and that the circumstances of its publication have not been traced. However, it was in 1642 that Urban VIII responded to petitions for an inquiry into the cause for the beatification of certain of the

English martyrs of whom, without doubt, the cardinal and the chancellor would stand at the head, immediately after the Carthusians.

Now the attribution to Holbein indicates that there was an original; the engraving is not the kind of hack likeness that would have been produced if no original had been available. Furthermore, Wyngaerde was a sufficiently competent artist to have made a much better job of copying the Holbein image as we know it, if that had been his original. There were, it should be remembered, quite a number of so-called Holbein portraits of More in or passing through Antwerp at this time, including the Rubens copy, the Orleans version, and others; the original of the family group may have gone via Antwerp on its way from the Arundel collection to the Imstenrädts. Any of these might have been the ultimate original.

Secondly, in 1675 there appeared at Milan the first edition of Domenico Regi's *Vita di Tomaso Moro*. It contains an engraved portrait clearly after (though not ascribed to) Holbein with the cap, the curl on the left temple, and the chain of SS accurately drawn, but differing from all previous portraits in much the same way as the Wyngaerde engraving—an opener brow and larger eyes. The figure is framed by two branches, one of palm and the other of laurel.[1] Finally—and this is a more curious coincidence—there is an engraved title, showing the fallen tree (now the laurel of immortal fame not the palm of martyrdom), with the axe embedded in the stump, and the legend SVAVIVS OLET. The engraving was copied several times and deteriorated considerably during the course of the several editions of Regi's work which appeared over the next fifty years, but the substantial details remain the same.

Thirdly, in 1679 Bishop Gilbert Burnet's *History of the Reformation* with a large engraving of More, not unlike that in Regi, but with a hooked nose, a more elaborate rendering of the chain of SS,[2] and the great purse which first appeared in Elstracke's engraving held in his hands. Under the frame appear the words 'H. Holben pinxit R. White sculpsit.' Although a more detailed and elaborate delineation, it is not so effective as Regi's. It nevertheless achieved some popularity and was often copied, as in Gregorio Leti's *Historia . . . di Eisabetta* (Amsterdam 1693).

Finally, there are a number of engravings which appear in several books by or about Erasmus and More between 1726 and 1740, all by Vertue and all said to be after Holbein, similar generally to the foregoing, but having the SS chain correctly drawn and a shade of moustache on More's upper lip, which was exaggerated by Houbraken and Cook when they copied Vertue's plate in 1742 and 1758.[3]

Now the compelling feature about all these engravings is that while they exhibit certain common features which are not found in any other engravings (notably the explicit attributions to Holbein), at the same time they differ from each other to an extent which excludes

---

[1] Compare the branches on either side of the title wording in the 1626 *Mirrour of Virtue*.

[2] It follows the pattern of Locky's version of the Family Group, but appears to derive its rather greater detail from a different source.

[3] These engravings appear in that indefatigable antiquarian Thomas Birch's collection of English portraits, *The Heads of Illustrious Persons* (London, 1743–51) and in Ferdinando Warner's *Memoirs of the Life of Thomas More* (London, 1758).

the possibility that some are copied from others. It might be supposed that an engraving for a popular Italian biography of a well-known Englishman might copy a contemporary popular English print. But no; the Italian print appears four years before the English. Again, Vertue would never have been satisfied with copying so slipshod a piece of work as White's engraving. We are forced then to the supposition that there was in existence, at least as early as the mid-seventeenth century, an image of More, with a more open brow and larger eyes—almost a smiling face (and possibly a softer cap), which was at that time ascribed to Holbein, when other engraved portraits were not. A small painting in oil on wood, presented by Dr Rawlinson to the Bodleian Library in 1755,[1] can also be placed in this group, and the original of a small anonymous stipple engraving of 1808, which is one of a number produced at that time, but is not, unlike the rest, based on the Bone miniatures of the Frick Portrait, the National Portrait Gallery version of the family group, or de Mechel's engraving of the family group drawing. 11 239

Various suggestions have been made as to the identity of Wyngaerde's original. What the North Italian original of the Regi engravings may have been is harder to say; it is possible that it was a miniature with a design on the reverse, like the bronze medallion, which would account for the recurrence of the SVAVIVS OLET legend and motif. It is even harder to guess at the original of White's engraving. None of the known 'Holbein' versions was bought or sold about this time, and the great collectors of earlier in the century who might have encouraged the engraver were all dead. It is, however, clearly derived from a Holbein-type original, though perhaps with some additions from Elstracke, possibly—the nose is curved—from one like the Bedford version. Vertue's original ought to be easier to find, since his travels in search of old pictures are so well documented. Unfortunately, though he mentions many portraits of More, he never says which he followed for his own engraving. It is tempting to suppose that he took the trouble to find an original of some authority, such as

an Antient picture—half lenght by Holbeen a piece always preserved in the family[2] 35

which he saw when he went to visit the Mores of Barnborough in 1728. But if so it, like so many of the pictures mentioned in the seventeenth and eighteenth centuries, including any picture which could be identified as in any way related to the original of this third group, has disappeared. There is the Holbein of More which von Sandrart (who should have known a Holbein when he saw one) found in Lord Arundel's long garden gallery, some time before 1628, but which does not appear in the inventory made in 1655 after Lord Arundel's death. There are a number mentioned in Vertue's notebooks, including some that were then considered to be old, which cannot now be identified. They may yet be found.

From now on the new portraiture of More is largely based on the recovery of originals which had lapsed from the public view. The best known example of this is the well-known stipple engraving by Bartolozzi based on the second Windsor drawing, which was included in John Chamberlaine's *Imitations of Original Drawings by Hans Holbein, in the Collection of* 237:40

[1] See Mrs R. L. Poole, *Catalogue of Oxford Portraits*, vol. i (1912), p. 10 (no. 23).
[2] *Notebooks*, II. 75. See above, p. 12.

His Majesty (London, 1792), a magnificent folio with the text printed by one of the most distinguished British printers, William Bulmer. Bartolozzi's is the only plate for more than a century which compares for skill or fidelity with Wyngaerde's line engraving. It is important, because it popularized a real Holbein portrait to such an extent that all the others were superseded; it became the standard portrait of More in the nineteenth century.

In the early years of the nineteenth century a great deal of interest was caused by the rediscovery of the Frick portrait (if such it was) and the Lenthall group now in the National Portrait Gallery, which came up for sale, though it was withdrawn, in 1808. The miniaturist Henry Bone made a number of enamel versions of the former, for which his design is in the National Portrait Gallery.[1] These miniatures were in their turn copied by engravers; one of the better examples is that engraved by R. Woodman for Knight's *Gallery of Portraits* (1824). The group too was much copied, though the engravings are mostly of indifferent quality; J. Thomson's, in *Lodge's Portraits* (1826) is one of the better examples.

The rediscovery of Holbein's sketch of the Family group was a trifle more eventful. It first appears, very indifferently etched by Charles Nicolas Cochin, in a curious medley of pictures put together by Carolina Patin under the title of *Tabellae Selectae* in 1691. She was the sister of the iconophile Dr Charles Patin, who probably found the sketch at the same time as the copy of Erasmus's *Moriae Encomium* with Holbein's famous marginal sketches, of which he published engraved facsimiles in his famous edition of 1676. It must have caused some stir, the more so as the location of the original and all the copies were not generally known. Vertue certainly knew of it before he had seen any of the pictures by or after Locky.[2] In 1726, among the many books of or about More and Erasmus put out at that time, the Reverend Dr Samuel Knight's *Life of Erasmus* was published, and facing page 310 was another engraving (a poor one, but, according to Dibdin, by Vertue) based on Cochin's etching. The result is a poor but not unimaginative and reasonably faithful copy, spoiled by the insertion of shading where the original has none. The plate was dedicated to Peter, Lord King (1669–1734), who married Locke's daughter and had just become Lord Chancellor. This was ten years after Hearne's edition of Roper had revived the memory of King's illustrious predecessor.

This engraving was copied very faithfully, dedication and all, in a German translation of the *Life of More* by his great-grandson Thomas More, which appeared in 1741, at Jena, of all places. The plate was engraved by the Leipzig craftsman Johann Benjamin Brühl (1691–1763). A print of the plate is to be found in the Guildhall Library where it forms an item in the collection of books and pictures relating to More assembled by Alfred Cock, late of the Middle Temple. He was a distinguished lawyer in his time, took silk in 1886, was a keen Positivist and Progressive, whom we should respect as a dedicated Utopian. Foreseeing his death, Cock decided to resolve his remains into carbolic acid, water and ammonia. He died in 1898 and was accordingly, as the phrase is, cremated—an 'advanced' decision to take

---

[1] See above, p. 9.
[2] He may have learned of it from Hearne's edition of Roper; in his preface Hearne, as well as quoting Rawlinson's long description of the Nostell version, mentions the Cochin engraving and its imperfections.

sixty years ago. As a memorial to this Utopian, Cock's library of Moreana was soon afterwards purchased by public subscription and presented to the City of London.

Finally the prolific engraver Christian de Mechel executed a number of copies in several media for his *Oeuvre de Jean Holbein* (Basel, 1780–95), including a pretty faithful line-engraving,[1] and some rather fanciful aquatint 'restorations' of the original, which he supposed to be in England, *in Anglia adservata*. He may have heard of one of the Locky originals: if so, he did not use it. Knight's engraving is a more probable source.

504

This brings us to the end of the history of the traditional portraiture of Thomas More. As indicated earlier, the popularity of Bartolozzi's engraving effectively put an end to any further divergence or variation in the likeness, and, as this popularity was caused by its likeness to one of the original Holbein portraits, the story may well be said to have come full circle. A less influential but nevertheless important factor in this more scholarly attitude was the publication in 1808 of the edition of *Utopia*, mentioned above, of that enthusiastic bibliophile, the Reverend Thomas Dibdin. It was splendidly printed by the same William Bulmer who printed Chamberlaine's *Illustrations*; it contained two engravings of More, and of his family, and woodcut decorations, after the edition of 1518, by Richard Austin; and among 180 pages of preliminary matter is the first list of portraits of More. Unfortunately, this is restricted to prints: only passing and incurious reference is made to their originals, in one or two cases. This may seem extraordinary, but it should be remembered that the fashion for prints was in its hey-day in 1808, and a detailed inquiry into original portraits would have seemed an impossible and pointless exercise.[2]

Dibdin based his list partly on the researches of William Bromley, the engraver, but much more on that immensely influential work, *A Biographical History of England, from Egbert the Great to the Revolution . . . adapted to a Methodical Catalogue of Engraved British Heads* (London 1769), by the Reverend James Granger, whose habit of enlarging his books by illustrations drawn from other sources added a new word to the English language. Dibdin, however, more than doubled Granger's list, and among the forty-one prints he listed, those that cannot be identified—only two or three—are due to Granger's imperfect descriptions. His most important achievement, however, was his understanding of the value of the Holbein original, and his estimation of the prints according to the nearness with which they corresponded to it. His own practice is less certain than his principle; while rejecting the most obvious, he seems, although doubtfully, to accept the series of prints based on the Brussels picture.[3] Nevertheless, Dibdin's was a pioneer work, and it is fitting that an account of the proper likeness of More should conclude with a word of gratitude for it. Although his *Utopia* cannot have enjoyed a wide circulation, it must have been read by those who most needed its influence, and Dibdin's insistence on the importance of the Holbein likeness made clear in cold print the lesson of Bartolozzi's engraving.

[1] It is inscribed 'Iohannes Holbein ad vivum delin: Londini 1530.', which provides the first independent evidence of the existence of the erroneous date added on the Basel sketch in a later hand; see above, pp. 20 and 22.

[2] More provoking is the entire absence of artist's name or provenance of the engraving which appears as the frontispiece to the work, which, as has been suggested (p. 65), is of some interest.

[3] See below, p. 69.

7. PORTRAITS NOT LIKENESSES

THE degree of variation to be found in the likenesses which we have already listed as portraits makes it difficult to select any single piece as a work of imagination. The distinction between a faithful depiction and an imaginary likeness would have been difficult for the sixteenth or seventeenth century mind to grasp.

701:7   The two woodcuts in Froben's edition of the *Utopia* (1518) are a case in point. While it is possible that Ambrosius Holbein knew his subjects by sight and could have achieved a genuine 'likeness', it is clear that he was not in any way concerned to do so, the more so perhaps since one of the characters, Hythlodaye, was in fact the work of imagination. All he needed to shew was the philosophical author of *Utopia*, not a speaking likeness of More

702   the man. The equally lively cuts in the Paris *Utopie* (1550) are still less concerned with More's real features. The 'execution' group of pictures again were chiefly designed to point a moral rather than delineate the man. The Amsterdam *Utopie* of 1643 has an engraved

703   title which shows a purely imaginary scene. Peter Gilles, Hythlodaye and More are shewn in contemporary dress sitting at a table in a formal garden whose geometric flowerbeds and carefully trained hedges (Dutch, clearly, and seventeenth century) stretch away behind them. A later engraving shows a Chancellor of sad mien set against a stone wall which evidently symbolizes the Tower. Finally, the fashion at the end of the eighteenth century

705   for 'historical' pictures produced a fine example of imaginative portraiture, William Hamilton's dramatic *The Parting of Sir Thomas More and his Daughter*.

AN ALLEGORICAL ENGRAVING AT GRAZ

Why was that part of Stapleton's *Tres Thomae* which deals with More reprinted at Graz in 1689? It was probably for the use of the famous Jesuit College there. Graz is far from any of the centres from which most of the portraits come, a fact demonstrated by the frontispiece

704:41   which gives a portrait of More which is no sort of likeness. It is, however, a most engaging romantic piece, of considerable quality. It is signed by Johannes Ulrich Kraus (1666–1719), a member of the well-known Augsburg family of artists. The portrait is an oval medallion, shewing a head and shoulders, a full, slightly melancholy face, with long hair, and a well-kempt moustache and small pointed beard. The doublet is buttoned up to the throat, in the fashion of the mid-century. The medallion is framed with a thick garland of mulberry leaves, on which silkworms are feeding, while full grown moths are seen flying near by. Below, on a stone bench, two female figures are seated, one gathering the leaves into a basket and detaching the cocoons, the other spinning the silk thread with the aid of a wheel and a distaff, at the point of which the allegorical eye of divine influence may be seen.

68

Holbein Delin.   Cochin Sculp.

1. Io: Morus, Thomæ pater, an. 76.
2. Anna Grisacria, Io. Mori sponsa, an. 15.
3. Thomas Morus, an. 50.
4. Alicia, Thomæ Mori uxor, an. 57.
5. Margarita Ropera, Th. Mori filia, an. 22.

FAMILIA THOMÆ MORI,
a Io: Holbenio delineata.
Tabella Patina

6. Elisabeta Damsæa, Th: Mori filia, an. 21.
7. Cæcilia Heronia, Th. Mori filia, an. 20.
8. Io. Morus, Th. filius, an. 19.
9. Margarita Giga, affinis, an. 22.
10. Henricus Patensonius, Th. Mori morio, an. 40.

Figure 38. Engraving by C. N. Cochin, 1691 (501)

Inscrib'd to the Rt. Honble PETER Ld. KING Ld. HIGH CHANCELLOR of Gread Britain.

Io: Morus Thomæ pater an.76.
Anna Crisacria Io:Mori Sponsa an:15.
Thomas Morus an:50.
Alicia Thomæ Mori Uxor an:57.
Margareta Ropera Tho.Mori filia an:22.

FAMILIA THOMÆ
MORI

6. Elizabetha Dauncia Tho Mori filia an.
7. Cecilia Heronia Tho:Mori filia an:20.
8. Io.Morus Tho: filius an:19.
9. Margareta Gige affinis an:22.
10. Henricus Patensonus Tho.Mori morio a

Figure 39. Engraving by Bruhl, 1741 (503)

From an Original Drawing by Hans Holbein

Engraved by F. Bartolozzi R.A. Historical Engraver to his Majesty

Publish'd as the Act directs Oct. 1. 1792. by J. Chamberlaine.

Figure 40. Aquatint by Bartolozzi, 1792 (237)

Figure 42. Engraving by Luke Vorstermann, 1631
(808)

Figure 41. Engraving by J. U. Kraus, in Stapleton
Vita Thomae Mori, Graz, 1689 (704)

Below are inscribed, in a flowery cartouche, four neat lines of verse, which play upon the Latin word for mulberry, *morus*, manners, *mores*, and *mori*, to die:

> Dat fructus homini, Bombyci serica morus.
> Virtuti, et Sophiae MORUS utrumque dabit
> Moribus e MORI texes tibi serica morum.
>   Si MORI Bombyx sedule, Lector, eris.

In other words, 'if you would be like More, read this book'.

The symbolism is so unusual, and the engraving so well done, that it sticks in the mind while more accurate portraits fade. It is perhaps not the least tribute to More's influence that 150 years after his death, in distant Austria, his biography should be capable of commanding such an original and delightful tribute.

THE SPURIOUS PORTRAITS

If it is hard to tell for certain which, of a number of the portraits, are poor likenesses, and which deliberately imaginary, it is easy enough to identify the spurious. One of the best known is the portrait by Holbein of Sir Thomas Wyatt in the Louvre, which was long 801 catalogued as More by Holbein. The most persistently mis-identified is a picture in the Musées Royaux des Beaux Arts at Brussels.[1] It is a small panel painting of a bearded man, 802 full face, half length, with a flat cap; in front of him is a small white dog sitting on a table. It too was long catalogued as More by Holbein; the most recent description calls it a portrait of an unknown man, and attributes it to Corneille de Lyon. The error goes back at least to 1631 when Luke Vorsterman made a fine engraving of it, with a legend which, 808:42 ironically enough, is the first to describe More as a martyr for religion in so many words; it runs: HEROA CERNIS? MORVS EST: FIDEI ILLE MARTYR OPTIMAE, KEIM-HΛION SAECLI SVI. And it was copied again and again. There is a fine example by Abraham Blooteling in the Dutch translation of *Utopia* (Amsterdam, 1677; copied in 1700), and by Esmé de Boullonois in Isaac Bullart's *Académie des Sciences et des Arts* (1682); another, very small, on the engraved title of Van der Aa's French translation of the *Utopia* (Leiden, 1715); it was copied again by E. Eichel; even as late as 1822, when the real Holbein likenesses were beginning to be well-known, an engraving of it was produced by Pye and said to be 'painted by Holbein'.

A false attribution of shorter duration is recorded by Horace Walpole.[2] When in Venice in 1741, he discovered that the famous Dresden version Holbein's picture of the Meyer 820 family praying to the Virgin and Child (the 'Darmstadt Madonna'), then in the Delfino palace, was, and had been since offered for sale to the Duke of Orleans in 1723, described as a portrait of the More family. Familiar with the authentic version, he realized the error and plausibly ascribed it to an Italian inability to distinguish between the German Meyer and the English More.

---

[1] No. 641.
[2] *Anecdotes of Painting in England*, ed. Wornum (London, 1888), vol. 1, p. 93.

Another portrait wrongly described as of Thomas More, of which probably more than

803   one example is known,[1] shows a figure three-quarter length, kneeling on a stool; it is probably of John Bourchier, 2nd Lord Berners. The confusion probably goes back to the seventeenth century. At the same period another, more ironic, confusion took place. In

804   1674 Mary More painted and presented to the Bodleian Library at Oxford a portrait said to be of Thomas More; it is in fact a fairly good copy of Holbein's portrait of Thomas

805   Cromwell, now in the Frick Collection. Another copy by Mary More is now in the Plympton Collection in New York, where it is still described as a portrait of More.

Two other portraits said to be of Sir Thomas More may be noted. One, sold at Sotheby's,

806   15 July 1953, appears to have been compounded in equal parts of Holbein's Cromwell and the Galle engraving of More. The other, in the Metropolitan Museum at New York, shews

807   a figure wearing the same cap and clothes as More in the Frick version. But the face is quite different: it has hollow cheeks, heavy eye-lids and sandy hair. It should be quite easy to identify the sitter, but it has not so far been done.

Finally, there are an extraordinarily large number of false engravings, some identifiable

809–12   as copies of known portraits of persons as diverse as Paracelsus and Rembrandt's father. One of the best of these—it was engraved by several craftsmen, including Christian de Mechel who should have known better—shews a burly, heavy-faced, thick-jowled sixteenth-century figure with a fur tippet and a pointed cap not unlike More's; but there the resemblance ceases. One of the oddest purports to be copied from a portrait of More by Titian in the Escorial. It is certainly not of More: the subject, bare-headed and bearded, suggests a late sixteenth- or early seventeenth-century date. It is equally unlikely that the original was by Titian. If there is a version further removed from Holbein's portrait of 1527, it has escaped this inquiry.

[1] One was sold at Christie's, 20 June 1919, lot 109; this or another also at Christie's, 16 July 1954, lot 32.

8. CONCLUSION

THE probable return of the Frick version to this country, Bartolozzi's engraving after the second Windsor drawing, Dibdin's fashionable edition of *Utopia*, the general revival of interest in Holbein, all these things mark a terminal point in the history of the portraiture of More. We have come full circle. The story began with the creation of the magnificent series of depictions, the drawings, the oil painting, the family group, by Holbein; it then diverged as the claims of the various qualities for which More stood exerted their influence on the manner in which he was depicted. Then the absence of any generally accepted and easily accessible authentic version caused a deterioration, punctuated by the appearance of certain likenesses with strong claims to be derived from an original of good quality; by contrast, it was at this time too that many of the allegorical and spurious representations came into being. Finally, the Holbein image is recovered and returns to dominate the subsequent portraiture of More.

Since then there has been no significant change. The persistence and vitality of the real, historical reporting of the Holbein image is one of the most astonishing features in the iconography of a man whose features were so frequently represented. Where the features of many of his contemporaries have been lost altogether, obscured by idealistic portraits, made the subject of doubts by conflicting versions, Holbein's image of More remains real and live, resisting the most determined efforts of second-rate engravers to disfigure and transform his features and attributes. We can, moreover, safely point to the great finished version in the Frick collection in the certainty that it is the first, most perfect and most authentic of all the surviving versions, and adduce the other versions and the relation suggested between them as proof.

It seems likely that More would have approved of this. His own views on the value and uses of portraits were clearly expressed and set out at the beginning of this survey. His passionate regard for the truth and dislike of any pretence would prefer the real likeness to any glorifications to be handed down to posterity.

When More wrote to Peter Gilles enclosing the letter from Erasmus quoted on the first page of this book, he sent him a little poem on the diptych by Matsys which deserves to be remembered here. The last lines, in which he is addressing the painter, may roughly be translated as follows.

> Why did you choose fragile wood to paint the portraits on,
> When you should have used a more faithful substance
> Which would have preserved them to eternity?
> Thus you could have made your own fame more sure

71

And fulfilled the wishes of posterity.
If the ages to come have any care
For the Arts, and cruel War does not
Extinguish Wisdom, how much may not posterity
Pay for this panel.[1]

[1] Erasmus: *Epistolae*, ed. Allen, vol. III, no. 684.

CATALOGUE

This list is necessarily incomplete. The present location of some of the portraits of More, and no doubt the existence of others, will elude this compilation. It is to be hoped, however, that its imperfections will encourage others to amplify and correct it. With this end in view, a number of early references to portraits of More, especially to those attributed to Holbein, have been included; although they do not appear, or cannot be proved, to refer to any of the portraits now known to exist, they may take on greater significance when further material comes to light.

I. SINGLE PORTRAITS OF MORE

A. Paintings and Drawings[1]

1. Royal collection, Windsor. Chalk drawing, with wash added later. $14\frac{15}{16} \times 10\frac{1}{8}$ inches. By Holbein.
    See pp. 16–18.
2. Royal collection, Windsor. Chalk drawing. $15\frac{13}{16} \times 11\frac{13}{16}$ inches. By Holbein.
    See pp. 16–18.
3. Frick collection, New York. Oil and tempera on wooden panel. $28\frac{7}{8} \times 23\frac{1}{4}$ inches. 'The Frick version.' By Holbein, 1527.
    See pp. 7–10.
4. Unlocated. 'The Orleans Version.'
    See pp. 12–13.
5. Unlocated. 'The Lumley Version.'
    See p. 13.
6. Collection of the Marquess of Lothian. Oil on panel. $29\frac{1}{2} \times 23$ inches. 'The Lothian Version.'
    See p. 13.
7. Private collection, Munich. Oil on panel. $29\frac{1}{2} \times 23$ inches. 'The Bedford Version.'
    See pp. 13–14.
8. Prado, Madrid. Oil on canvas. $41\frac{1}{2} \times 28\frac{3}{4}$ inches. Free copy by Peter Paul Rubens.
    See p. 62.
9. Unlocated. Oil on panel. $29 \times 23\frac{1}{2}$ inches. From the collection of Richard Tayloors, sold at Sotheby's, 27 April 1960, lot 92.
    See p. 14.
10. Oriel College, Oxford. Canvas. $29 \times 24\frac{1}{2}$ inches. Presented in 1787 by Dr Rawbone.
11. Bodleian Library Oxford. Panel 10×8 inches. Bequeathed by Richard Rawlinson in 1755. Without curl on left cheek.
    See p. 65.
12. Corpus Christi College, Cambridge. Panel. $22\frac{7}{8} \times 17\frac{3}{8}$ inches. A late seventeenth-century

---

[1] Portraits in this section still known to be in existence may be assumed, unless otherwise indicated, to be related to the Holbein single portrait.

version, possibly derived from a Family Group portrait; SS chain in some detail, the thick strokes of the S in open work. One of a group of similar portraits of famous men of the sixteenth and seventeenth centuries (see nos. 23 and 47).

13. Collection of Major H. E. J. Spearman, London. Panel. 30½ × 25¼ inches. From the collection of Sir Hugh Cholmeley.

14. Grey-Egerton collection, Oulton Park. Canvas. 28¾ × 24½ inches. First recorded in an inventory of 1732. Exhibited Manchester 1857 (Portraits, no. 338). Possibly destroyed in the Oulton fire in 1926.
See *Descriptive Catalogue . . . Oulton Park*, 1884, pp. 18–20.

15. Collection of Earl Spencer, Althorp. Canvas. 30 × 25 inches, approx. First recorded in 1762; in the 1851 Althorp catalogue. Without collar of SS.

16. Collection of Lord Sackville, Knole. Canvas. 28½ × 22½ inches. Long catalogued as by David Mytens after Holbein. Without collar of SS.

17. The Speaker's House, Westminster. Canvas. 23 × 19½ inches. Late copy, head and shoulders only, inscribed: *Given by the Rt. Honble Charles Abbot 1803*.
See A. J. Dasent, *Speakers of the House of Commons*, 1911, p. 122 (reproduced).

18. National Portrait Gallery, London (3543). Panel. 21⅞ × 16½ inches. From the collection of the Earl of Ellenborough, sold at Sotheby's, 11 June 1947.

19. Collection of Lord Sackville, Knole. Panel. A good, probably sixteenth-century, copy; clearly based on a 'single portrait' version, although the face suggests the 'Group version'. The chain is accurately rendered, showing 22 left and SS right, a cross replacing the rose. More's left hand rests on a book, on which there is a faded inscription . . . VT S . . . . SED CAVSA.

20. Collection of J. R. More-Molyneux, Loseley Park. Panel. An early copy, perhaps sixteenth century.

21. Miniature versions by Henry Bone, *c*. 1810, apparently after the Frick version.
    (*a*) Squared-off drawing in the National Portrait Gallery Archives, London.
    (*b*) In the possession of Thomas Clarke, engraved from an 'enamel after Holbein' by R. Woodman, *c*. 1820.
    (*c*) In the collection of the Duke of Buccleuch.
    (*d*) Seen by C. Stryienski, *c*. 1900, dated 1811, supposedly after an original at Todi.
    (*e*) In the collection of Charles Robertson of Batworth Park in 1935 (7 × 5½ inches).
    (*f*) Once in the collection of the Earl of Shrewsbury, and sold at the Alton Towers Sale in 1857.
    See pp. 9, 65 and 66.

22. National Portrait Gallery, London (306). Panel 28 × 23 inches. Bought from W. Dyer, a London dealer, June 1870. Possibly derived from the Family Group portrait.

23. Collection of Lord Sackville, Knole. Panel 30 × 25 inches, approx. Probably by John Belcamp, one of a series of famous men at Knole painted by him in the seventeenth century. Probably based on the *Herω-ologia* engraving.

24. Collection of Col. Parker, Clitherowe, Yorkshire. Panel. Damaged, but some resemblance to the Holkham version, 25.

25. Collection of the Earl of Leicester, Holkham Hall. Canvas. 37½ × 40 inches. Three-quarter length, standing.
See p. 62.

26. Versailles. Canvas. Half length. Perhaps after *Herω-ologia* engraving.
    See p. 55.

27. Collection of the Duke of Beaufort, Badminton. Panel. 30¼ × 22 inches.
    See p. 61.

28. Eyston Collection, East Hendred. Canvas. 16 × 11 inches.
    See pp. 11–12.

29. Unlocated. Lent by Sir Thomas Baring to the British Institution in 1820 (no. 118) as of More by Holbein.

30. Unlocated. Panel. 28 × 18 inches. Seen by Vertue at the Rt. Honble. Speaker Onslow's 'a picture of Sir Tho. More Kᵗ Chancellor of England' (*Notebooks*, V, 32).

31. Unlocated. In Vernon collection at Sudbury in 1796 (B.M. Add. MS. 6391, f.26, no. 27), presumably sold at Vernon Sale, Christie's, 15 June 1844.

32. Unlocated. Seen by Vertue at 'Weston, Warwickshire . . . Mr Sheldons in the great Room' (*Notebooks*, IV, 140).

33. Poulett collection, Hinton St George. Recorded in 1742 (B.M. Add. MS. 6391, f. 178, no. 29).

34. Unlocated. Panel. Seen by Vertue at 'Sr John Gaudy'; 'there was also a picture of Sr Tho More on bord—bensˢ' (*Notebooks*, IV, 14).

35. Unlocated. Panel. Seen by Vertue at Barnborough.
    See pp. 11–12, 65.

36. Unlocated. Panel 22½ × 17 inches. Head and shoulders only, inscribed at top: SYR THOMAS MOUR LORD CHANCLER OF ENGLANDE. Sold at Sotheby's, 25 March 1936, lot 84.

37. Unlocated. Sold in London, 25 March 1772, lot 85 ('A Nobleman, from his seat in Nottinghamshire').

38. Unlocated. Sold in London, 25 February 1775, lot 67 ('Gansell').

39. Unlocated. Sold at Christie's, 11 August 1785, lot 15.
    See p. 13.

40. Unlocated. Sold in London, 26 March 1790, lot 59 ('Chauncey').

41. Unlocated. Sold at Greenwood's, 31 March 1791, lot 84 ('A Gentleman's').

42. Unlocated. Sold at Dawson's, 18 December 1807, lot 20.
    See p. 13.

43. Unlocated. Canvas. 21 × 17 inches. Half length, to right, hands resting on book, and holding scroll inscribed '*Henricus Rex 1532 pinx 1532*'. Exhibited Tudor Exhibition, London, 1890, (no. 127, lent by T. L. Thurlow) and Manchester (no. 59, lent by Miss Sumner).

44. Unlocated. In the possession of Nicolaes Cornelis Cheeus at Antwerp in 1622, where it was paired with a portrait of Erasmus. Both pictures were inherited by Anna de Schot from Cheeus's widow (inventory of 21 April 1663).
    See J. Denucé, *The Antwerp Art Galleries in the Seventeenth Century*, pp. 30, 238.

45. Unlocated. In the collection of Jeremias Wildens in 1652.
    See J. Denucé, op. cit., p. 167.

46. Unlocated. Listed in the inventory of the pictures of Cornelia van Vinckenborch in 1681.
    See J. Denucé, op. cit., p. 304.

47. Unlocated. Noted by Vertue among a number of pictures ('heads only') attributed to John Belcamp brought by Edward Harley, Earl of Oxford, from Wimpole Hall to his house in London, by 1736. These pictures had previously belonged to Sir Henry Pickering and before

that to the Tempest family; the names of the subjects were 'writ on a piece of paper pasted on the back of each picture mostly' (*Notebooks*, IV, 167).

48. Unlocated. Canvas. 'Sir Thomas More his picture on cloth ¾ a scroll in his hand—a picture of him that might be something different from that of his great portraits by H. Holbein in poses. Mr Yeates' (Vertue, *Notebooks*, V, 12).

49. Unlocated. Panel. 12⅝ × 11 inches. Reported in a private collection in Montreal and attributed to Dürer in *Sint Lucas* (Amsterdam and Brussels), IV (1911), 2, p. 60; see Veth-Muller, *Dürer's Niederländische Reise*, vol. II, p. 244. Clearly a late copy of the Holbein single portrait.

50. Musée des Beaux-Arts, Brussels. Panel. Attributed to Jean Gossaert de Maubeuge; probably after a good early copy, the chain of SS being accurately rendered.

51. Couvent du Gesu, Brussels. Panel. Double portrait of More (without chain) and Fisher (a poor likeness); probably seventeenth century.

52. Unlocated. Reported by Joachim von Sandrart in the collection of Thomas Howard, Earl of Arundel, *c.* 1625–7. See p. 11.

53. Collection of the Marquess of Bath, Longleat. Panel. 29½ × 24 inches.

54. Chichester–Constable Collection, Burton Constable. Panel. 29 × 24 inches.

55. Collection of the Dowager Duchess of Norfolk, Everingham Hall.

56. Unlocated. Panel, once in the collection of the Rt. Hon. John Burns; exhibited at the More Memorial Exhibition at Chelsea in July 1929, and attributed to Hans Eworth.

57. Unlocated. Panel 28 × 22½ inches. Once in the collection of the Earl of Shrewsbury and sold at the Alton Towers sale in 1847; later in the Burdett-Coutts collection and sold at Christie's, 4–5 May 1922 (bought by Vicars).

58. Unlocated. Panel. 17 × 15 inches. Sold at Christie's, 12 February 1926.

59. Unlocated. Panel. 13 × 10 inches. From the collection of P. C. F. Tatham, sold at Christie's, 5 July 1926.

60. Unlocated. Panel 28¼ × 21¼ inches. Sold at Christie's, 4 July 1930.

61. Unlocated. Panel. 28½ × 23 inches. From the collection of Sir John Ramsden, sold at Christie's, 27 May 1932.

62. Unlocated. Panel. 17 × 13½ inches. Sold at Christie's, 9 May 1934 (a doubtful attribution).

63. Unlocated. Sold at Piot Sale, Paris, 1864.

64. Collection of the Hon. Clive Pearson, Parham.

65. Collection of the Earl of Scarborough, Lumley.
    See p. 15.

66. Unlocated. Listed in the inventory of Cardinal Philip Howard in 1694.
    See p. 15.

67. Unlocated. Seen by Cole at 'the English Benedictines' in Paris, 1866.
    See p. 15.

68. Unlocated. A copy of 'a fine Holbein' given to Sir George Richmond by 'Dr Page' in 1855.

69. Harvard University, Law School.

70. In the collection of Lord Cornwallis, Brome Hall, 1780; 'called Sir Thomas More, of the time of Holbein; and his Lady its companion'.

71. In the collection of the Duke of Queensberry, Amesbury, *c.* 1800; from 'Lord Chancellor Clarendon', one of a group of portraits. Compare nos. 23 and 47.

72. Unlocated. Exhibited at the British Institution, 1840, lent by 'the late Mr. Carr'.

73. In the collection of Lord Melbourne, Brocket Hall, *c.* 1820.

74. In the collection of the Marquess of Northampton, Castle Ashby, *c.* 1820.

75. In the Weld collection, Ince, *c.* 1857. Described by Waagen, *Galleries and Cabinets of Art*, p. 252, as old and on board.

76. In the De Clifford collection, King's Weston, in 1796. 'A small head.'

77. Collection of Lord Hastings, Melton Constable. A portrait of Frick type, but 'half of a little smooth white dog with a gold collar is apparent on the left side' (Prince Frederick Duleep Singh, *Portraits in Norfolk Houses*, 1908, vol. II, p. 40).

78. In the collection of Lord le Despencer, *c.* 1825.

79. In the collection of Sir George Clerk, Penicuik, *c.* 1820.

80. In the collection of Lord Arundell, Wardour Castle, 1797.

81. In the Hardwick collection, Wimpole Hall, 1798. Noted, *c.* 1815, by G. P. Harding as 'by Holbein'.

82. In the collection of the Earl Waldegrave, Strawberry Hill, *c.* 1820.

83. In the collection of Mr Skynner, *c.* 1863. On board, with cradle. Clearly based on a version of the family group; possibly an early nineteenth-century copy of the National Portrait Gallery version (404).

84. In the Bouverie collection, Beechnorth, Surrey, *c.* 1825.

85. In the collection of the Duke of Norfolk, Graystock, *c.* 1825.

86. In the Arden collection, Harden Hall, Cheshire, *c.* 1825.

B. *Miniature Portraits*

101. Lincoln's Inn, London. Watercolours on vellum. Circular, $2\frac{3}{8}$ inches diameter,
See p. 30.

102. Cleveland Museum of Art, Ohio. Oil on wood panel. Circular, $2\frac{9}{16}$ inches diameter.
See p. 30.

103. Collection of the Duke of Buccleuch. Oil, probably on gesso on a silver plaque. Oval, $1\frac{5}{16} \times 1\frac{1}{4}$ inches.
See p. 32.

104. Collection of Mr Stanley Morison. Gouache on vellum. $3\frac{5}{8} \times \frac{5}{8}$ inches.
See pp. 59–60.

105. Cock collection, Guildhall, London. Oil on panel. $3\frac{1}{16} \times 2\frac{5}{8}$ inches. A late seventeenth- or early eighteenth-century version, probably based on a larger picture. Trace of moustache and —unusually—SS on left and ƧƧ on right of chain.

106. Cock collection, Guildhall, London. Coloured wax bas-relief. 5×4 inches. By Casella. Some resemblance to Bone enamels, possibly related to 'Wax medallion', no. 1412, Tudor Exhibition, London 1890.

107. Unlocated. Watercolours. In the possession of the Mores of Barnborough in 1728.
See pp. 32–3.

108. Unlocated. Wood panel. Circular, 4 inches diameter. In the collection of Charles I.
See pp. 30–2.

109. Unlocated. Oil. Noted by Evelyn in the collection of Sir William Ducy; possibly not a miniature.
See p. 32.

110. Unlocated. Exhibited South Kensington Museum, 1862 (no. 2458, lent by Sir W. T. Holburne); not in catalogue of 1865 exhibition.

111. Unlocated. Lent by 'the Jesuit Fathers' to the More Memorial Exhibition (1929); described as 'of uncertain date'.

112. Unlocated. In oils on copper. Lent by Charles Robertson (see no. 21e) to the More–Fisher Exhibition at Oxford (1935).

C. Prints

This list is as far as possible complete up till 1700: after that date, only the more important prints have been recorded, though some of the commoner derivatives of them have also been noted.

201. Woodcut. Oval $2\frac{5}{16} \times 2$ inches. Published by John Fowler, 1568.
See pp. 47–8.

202. Engraving. $5\frac{1}{2} \times 4\frac{7}{8}$ inches. Published in Philip Galle, *Virorum Doctorum . . . Effigies*, Antwerp, 1572.
See pp. 49–50.

203. Woodcut. Circular $1\frac{5}{8}$ inches diameter. Published in Antoine du Verdier, *La Prosopographie*, Lyon, 1573.
See p. 48.

204. Woodcut. $4\frac{1}{4} \times 3\frac{3}{16}$ inches. By Tobias Stimmer; first published in P. Giovio, *Elogia virorum litteris eruditorum*, Basel, 1577.
See p. 61.

205. Woodcuts. Circular $1\frac{7}{16}$ inches diameter. Possibly by Reverdy; first published in *Promptuarii iconum insigniorum . . . pars secunda*, Rouille, Lyon 1578.
See p. 50.

206. Engraving. $5\frac{1}{8} \times 4\frac{3}{8}$ inches. Reverse copy of no. 202.
See p. 50.

207. Engraving. $6\frac{3}{4} \times 5\frac{1}{2}$ inches. Published in André Thévet, *Vie des Hommes Illustres*, Paris, 1584.
See p. 50.

208. Engraving. $4 \times 2\frac{9}{16}$ inches. Published in Thomas Stapleton, *Tres Thomae*, Douai, 1588.
See p. 61.

209. Engraving. $5\frac{5}{8} \times 4\frac{1}{8}$ inches. By R. Boissard; published in *Icones Virorum Illustrium*, Frankfurt, 1598.
See p. 50.

210. Engraving. $3\frac{9}{16} \times 2\frac{9}{16}$ inches. By Anton Wiericx.[1]
See pp. 51–3.

211. Woodcut. Circular, $1\frac{1}{4}$ inches diameter. Published in V. Andreas, *Imagines doctorum virorum*, Antwerp, 1611.
See p. 53n.

[1] See footnote on p. 79.

212. Engraving. $4\frac{5}{16} \times 3\frac{1}{16}$ inches. By John Faber. Published in *Utopia*, Leipzig, 1612.

See p. 53.

213. Engraving. $6\frac{1}{4} \times 4\frac{5}{8}$ inches. Probably by Willem or Magdalena van de Passe. Published in Henry Holland *Herω-ologia Anglica*, Arnhem, 1620.

See pp. 53–5.

214. Engraving. $7\frac{3}{8} \times 4\frac{1}{2}$ inches. By Renold Elstracke.

See pp. 56–7.

215. Engraving. $2\frac{7}{8} \times 2\frac{3}{8}$ inches. By Jean Valdor, 1621. Another state, with an entirely different inscription to Gosuinus Batsonicus, is also known.

See pp. 55–6.

216. Engraving. $4\frac{1}{4} \times 2\frac{3}{8}$ inches. Reverse copy of 215; published in W. Roper, *The Mirrour of Vertue*, St Omer, 1626.[1]

See pp. 57–8.

217. Etching. $8\frac{1}{16} \times 6\frac{1}{8}$ inches. Enlarged copy of 213. Unsigned.

See pp. 55.

218. Engraving. $3\frac{1}{2} \times 2\frac{1}{2}$ inches. By 'Cd'.

See p. 55.

219. Engraving. $3\frac{3}{8} \times 2\frac{3}{8}$ inches. In B.M. MS. Harley 6254.

See p. 58.

220. Engraving. $4\frac{1}{16} \times 2\frac{1}{2}$ inches. By W. Marshall. Published as title page to *Epigrammata Thomae Mori*, London, 1638. The same plate with the title and imprint altered appeared as title page to *Utopia*, London, 1639.

See p. 58.

221. Engraving. $5\frac{7}{16} \times 4\frac{3}{16}$ inches. By B. Moncornet, 1654. A good copy of 215.

222. Engraving. $\frac{11}{16} \times \frac{11}{16}$ inches. Part of engraved title to John Cotgrave, *Wit's Interpreter*, London, 1655.

See p. 57.

223. Engraving. $1\frac{3}{16} \times 1$ inches. Part of engraved title to Thomas Bayley (ed.), *Witty Apophthegmes* London, 1658.

See p. 57.

224. Engraving. 7×5 inches. By Frans van den Wyngaerde, supposedly after Holbein.

See pp. 63–4.

225. Engraving. Oval, $4 \times 3\frac{3}{16}$ inches. Copy of the figure only of 224, in oval frame, probably dating from the end of the century.

226. Engraving. $5\frac{9}{16} \times 2\frac{7}{8}$ inches. First published in D. Regi, *Della Vita di Thomaso Moro*, Milano, 1675; reversed and re-reversed copies found in subsequent editions.

See p. 64.

227. Engraving. $9\frac{3}{4} \times 5\frac{7}{8}$ inches. By R. White, supposedly after Holbein. First published in G. Burnet, *The History of the Reformation*, London 1679. A poor copy was included in the *Abridgement* of this work in 1683. It was also copied (engraving by P. Sims and an anonymous etching) *c.* 1800–1820.

See p. 64.

---

[1] Both these engravings were faithfully copied by steel-engraving for S. W. Singer's edition of Roper's *Life of More* in 1817.

228. Engraving. $2\frac{7}{8} \times 1\frac{3}{4}$ inches. Published in P. Freher, *Theatrum Virorum eruditione clarorum*, Nürnberg, 1688.
See p. 58.

229. Engraving. $11 \times 6\frac{7}{8}$ inches. Published in *Thomae Mori Opera Omnia*, Frankfurt, C. Gensch, 1689.
See p. 50.

230. Engraving. $4\frac{3}{4} \times 2\frac{7}{8}$ inches. Published in G. Leti, *Historia di Elisabetta*, Amsterdam, 1693; copies in subsequent editions.
See p. 64.

231. Engraving. $6\frac{1}{2} \times 5\frac{5}{8}$ inches, excluding frame. By P. S. van Gunst after A. van de Werfft; published in I. de Larrey, *Histoire d'Angleterre*, Rotterdam, 1697–8.
See p. 58.

232. Engraving. $5\frac{11}{16} \times 3\frac{5}{16}$ inches. By E. Desrochers, *c.* 1700. A good engraving, freely copied from no. 215 or no. 216.

233. Engraving. $6\frac{1}{2} \times 3\frac{11}{16}$ inches. By Michael Burghers. Published in W. Roper *Vita . . . Mori*, ed. T. Hearne, Oxford 1716.
See p. 58.

234. Engraving. $7 \times 4\frac{5}{8}$ inches. Half length, holding book, published as part of a double portrait (More and Erasmus) in *Utopia*, Frankfurt, 1704. Copied in *Encomium della Pazza*, Basel, 1761.

235. Engraving. $6\frac{5}{8} \times 3\frac{7}{8}$ inches. By G. Vertue, supposedly after Holbein. Published in several versions and sizes in editions of Erasmus, *The Praise of Folly* and W. Roper, *Life of More* between 1726 and 1740. Copied by Brühl, Houbraken, Cook, Audinet, Grignion and others up to *c.* 1775.
See p. 64.

236. Engraving. $4\frac{1}{4} \times 2\frac{3}{8}$ inches. By T. Kitchin. *c.* 1760. A very poor full length, possibly based on Houbraken.

237. Stipple. $16\frac{1}{2} \times 11\frac{3}{8}$ inches. By F. Bartolozzi, after the 'second' Windsor drawing (2). Copies by Cheesman, R. Scriven (for the second edition of Singer's edition of Roper's *Life* in 1822) and many others.
See pp. 65–6.

238. Stipple. $12\frac{3}{4} \times 9\frac{3}{8}$ inches. A large allegorical piece designed to illustrate R. Bowyer's edition of Hume's *History of England*, 1795, by R. Smirke and engraved by Newton and Parker. It shews a muse standing at the foot of a palm tree, her hand resting on a plinth marked STATESMEN; from the branches of the palm hang oval medallion busts of Thomas Cromwell, Cardinals Pole and Wolsey and More (likeness based on Houbraken), and on the ground are others of Thomas Howard, Duke of Norfolk, the Earl of Leicester and Sir Francis Walsingham.

239. Stipple $4\frac{1}{8} \times 3\frac{3}{8}$ inches. Published by W. Miller, 1808.
See p. 65.

240. Mezzotint. $5\frac{1}{2} \times 4$ inches. By C. Turner 'from a drawing by Bulfinch after Holbein'; published by S. Woodburn, 1811. A similar engraving also exists.

241. Engraving. $5 \times 3\frac{7}{8}$ inches. By R. Woodman 'from an enamel in the possession of Thomas Clarke, Esq.'; published in Knight's *Gallery of Portraits*, London, 1824.
See p. 66.

242. Stipple. $7\frac{3}{8} \times 5\frac{7}{8}$ inches. By J. Thomson after a drawing by W. Derby 'after the Holbein in the collection of W. J. Lenthall, Esq. December 24, 1823'. Published in *Lodge's Portraits*, London, 1826. Copied by Dean and others.

243. Lithograph. $12\frac{1}{4} \times 9\frac{1}{4}$. By G. Sensi after Rubens (8), Madrid, 1858.

244. Engraving. $4\frac{3}{4} \times 2\frac{3}{16}$ inches. Published in *Apollinis Judicium* ('Messina', 1672); full length, of uncertain origin.

II. MEDALLIONS OF MORE

301. Bronze. Diameter, 60 mm. Obv: profile portrait bust, inscribed THOMAS MORVS ANGLIAE CANCELL. Rev: a newly felled tree, an axe embedded in the stamp, inscribed SVAVIVS OLET.
    See pp. 34–6.

301A. Etching after the above. $7\frac{1}{4} \times 3\frac{1}{2}$ inches (plate-mark), shewing both obverse and reverse. Unsigned, but a pencilled attribution on the example in the Print Room of the British Museum reads 'Etched by Lees . . . from a medal said to be unique.'

302. Silver. Diameter, 37.5 mm. Obv.: portrait of More, head and shoulders, facing left, inscribed EFFIGIES THOMAE MORI MARTIRIS ANGLI. Rev: portrait of St Thomas à Becket head and shoulders, facing right, mitred, holding cross in right hand and book in left, inscribed S. THOMAS ARCHIEP. CANTVAR. MART. AN. 1171.
    See p. 55.

III. PORTRAITS OF THE MORE FAMILY GROUP

A. Paintings and Drawings

401. Unlocated, probably destroyed. Probably watercolour ('distemper') on cloth, approximately life-size. By Holbein, 1527.
    See pp. 18–20.

402. Kunstmuseum, Basel. Pen and ink drawing on paper. $15\frac{1}{4} \times 20\frac{5}{8}$ inches. By Holbein, 1527 or 1528.
    See pp. 20–1.

403. Collection of Lord St Oswald, Nostell Abbey. Oil on canvas. 99×138 inches. By Rowland Locky, signed, after Holbein, about 1590.
    See pp. 22–3.

404. National Portrait Gallery, London. Oil on canvas. $89\frac{1}{2} \times 131\frac{1}{2}$ inches. By Rowland Locky. in part after Holbein, 1593.
    See pp. 22–3.

405. Private collection, Great Britain. Watercolours, probably on vellum. $9\frac{1}{2} \times 11\frac{1}{2}$ inches, Attributed to Rowland Locky, about 1590.
    See pp. 23–4.

406. Eyston family collection, East Hendred. Canvas. 92× 117½ inches. Possibly mid-seventeenth century, after Locky.
See p. 24.
407. Chelsea Society, London, Canvas. 99× 134 inches.
See p. 24.
408. W. H. M. Vane, Esq., Hutton in the Forest. Canvas. 55× 48 inches.
See p. 24.

B. Engravings

501. Etching. 11⅛× 14½ inches. By C. N. Cochin after Holbein's pen and ink sketch (402). Published in Caroline Patin *Tabellae Selectae,* Padua and Cologne, 1691.
See p. 66.
502. Engraving. 6⅜× 7⅜. inches. Published in S. Knight, *The Life of Erasmus,* Cambridge, 1726.
See p. 66.
503. Engraving. 6⅜× 7 inches. Signed 'Bruhl sc. Lips.'. Published in *Das Leben des Sir Thomas More,* Leipzig, 1741.
See p. 66 and no. 234 above.
504. Etching. 14⅛× 19¼ inches. By Christian de Mechel, 1787, after the Basel sketch. De Mechel also executed another engraving and two other copies in aquatint with added shading. The engraving was copied by W. Poole for Dibdin's edition of *Utopia* (1808), and this was in turn copied by several engravers. One of them, Lewis, also did a copy in water-colours (formerly in the Burns collection).
See p. 67.

See also nos. 22, 83 and 242 above.

IV. PICTURES OF MORE IN PRISON, AND OF HIS EXECUTION

601. Woodcuts. 8¼× 5½ inches and 3⅜× 5½ inches. In *Ein Glaubwirdige Anzaygung des Tods Hernn Thome Mori* (Augsburg?), 1536.
See p. 41.
602. Miniature. 4½× 3 inches. Gouache. In British Museum Add. MS 28786, f4.
See pp. 41–2.
603. Destroyed *c.* 1800. Fresco by Niccolò Circignani, il Pomarancio, *c.* 1580.
See pp. 42–4.
604. Engraving after 603. By G. B. Cavalieri. In *Ecclesiae Anglicanae Trophaea,* Rome, 1584.
See pp. 42, 44–5.
605. Unlocated. Possibly after 603. Noted by Sir George Scharf as in the Barberini Palace in 1887.
See p. 45n.
606. Musée de Blois. 45½× 56¼ inches. By Antoine Caron.
See pp. 45–6.

607. Engraving. 4× 5⅜ inches. In Richard Verstegan, *Theatrum Crudelitatum Haereticorum*, Antwerp, 1592.
See p. 45.

608. Unlocated. Once in the possession of Margaret Clement and shewn by her to Thomas Stapleton.
See p. 42.

609. Unlocated. By Mattia Preti.
See p. 62n.

610. Unlocated, but possibly in the Escorial, Madrid. Listed in the 1587 inventory of the portrait-collection of Philip II as of More *en el cadahalco*. See p. 46.

611. Unlocated. Once in the possession of Sir Hans Sloane, and recorded as being in crayons and by Holbein, and dated 'June 1535'. See p. 46.

V. PORTRAITS OF MORE NOT LIKENESSES

A. Imaginative Portraits

701. Two woodcuts in *Utopia*, Basel, 1518. Both shew More with the other characters of the book, first in front of a map of Utopia, and secondly in the garden of More's house in Bruges. See pp. 5, 68.

702. Two woodcuts in the French translation, *L'Utopie*, Paris, 1550. The first is a conversation piece, the second shews More in his study, writing; probably based on 701.
See p. 68.

703. Engraving, title page to *L'Utopie*, Amsterdam, 1643. Another conversation piece in a garden.
See p. 68.

704. Engraving, by J. U. Kraus, frontispiece to Thomas Stapleton, *Vita Thomae Mori*, Graz, 1689.
See pp. 68-9.

705. Unlocated. Oil painting, *The Parting of Sir Thomas More and his daughter*, by William Hamilton; engraved by Robert Meadows for Macklin, 1 April 1790. Based on Holbein.
See p. 68.

B. Spurious Portraits

801. Louvre, Paris. Painting of Sir Henry Wyatt by Holbein, long catalogued as More. P. Ganz, *The Paintings of Hans Holbein the Younger*, London, 1950. p. 233, no. 50 and pl. 87, and see p. 69 above.

802. Musées Royaux des Beaux Arts, Brussels (no. 641). Small panel of bearded man with a small dog on a table before him; possibly by Corneille de Lyon.
See p. 69.

803. Unlocated. Portrait of John Bourchier, 2nd Lord Berners, three-quarter length, kneeling at a stool, inscribed SIR THOMAS MORE. See Waagen, *Galleries and Cabinets of Art in Great Britain*, 1857, p. 464, and p. 70 above.

804. Bodleian Library. Portrait of Thomas Cromwell, Earl of Essex, derived from Holbein's portrait in Frick Collection; painted and presented to Oxford in 1674 by Mary More, as a portrait of More, see Mrs A. L. Poole, *Catalogue of Portraits . . . Oxford*, i, p. 11 (no. 27), 1912.

See p. 69.

805. Plympton collection. As 804 above, with inscription on scroll as Thomas More and inscribed *Maria More Pinx 1574* (*sic*). Sold at Christie's, 5 April 1929, lot 48.

See p. 69.

806. Unlocated. Unknown man, head and shoulders to right, on panel 18¼ × 13 inches, catalogued as 'said to be St Thomas More' and sold at the Ashburnham Sale, Sotheby's, 15 July 1953, lot 144. Curious resemblance both to Holbein's Cromwell and the Galle engraving.

807. Metropolitan Museum, New York. Unknown man, half length to left, cap and clothes as Frick version, clasps vertical scroll in right hand, but features quite different.

808. Engraving, by Luke Vorstermann, based on 802. Copied by A. Blooteling and many others.

See p. 69.

809. Engravings, 'RH inven: R. Gaywood fecit. P. Stent excudit'. Based on Rembrandt's etching of his father. Another version by François Langlois also exists.

810. Engravings, of a man in sixteenth-century dress, 'with a fat jowl, bulbus nose, and frizzled wig' (Dibdin, no. 35, pp. cxxxvi), by T. Holloway and Christian de Mechel (*ad picturam I: Holbenii Londini prostantem*) and others, for editions of Lavater's *Physiognomy*.

811. Engraving, by F. Muntaner after L. Bueno, of a portrait, said to be of More by Titian, in the Escorial.

See p. 70.

812. Engraving, by J. M. Will, of full length figure in chair, long hair and skull-cap, table to right with books; possibly derived from a portrait of Paracelsus.

813. Unlocated. Half length to right, on canvas 17½ × 13½ inches, lent by Baroness Burdett-Coutts to Tudor Exhibition, London, 1890 (no. 161); reference in description to the subject's 'beard' suggests a derivative of 802. Sold at Burdett-Coutts Sale, Christie's, 4–5 May 1922.

814. Aix-en-Provence (No. 283). Head and shoulders, bespectacled face looking down at book; from the Entrecasteaux and Fabregoulles de Bourguignon collections, said to be by Holbein, 1539.

815. Unlocated. Sold at Shirley Sale, Stratford-on-Avon, 29–31 October 1946, lot 846 (Knight, Frank and Rutley). Described as More by Holbein, but clearly not.

816. Gardner Collection, Boston. Half length, to left; described as More by Dürer. The dress of the subject suggests a German origin, possibly later in the sixteenth century. A similar portrait is in the royal collection at Hampton Court.

817. Collection of H. J. R. Bankes, Kingston Lacy, Dorset. Exhibited R.A. Old Masters Exhibition, 1892, as More.

818. Unlocated, possibly at Milan. Portrait of a young bearded man, in early seventeenth-century dress; exhibited Thomas More Exhibition, Brussels, 1962, no. 144.

819. Alister Mathews Ltd, Poole, Dorset. Pastel on canvas, mounted on board. 13 × 9⅞ inches. signed and dated 'E. S. [?] 1709'. A note on the back indicates that it was given by R. P. Daniell to the Rev. W. Read in 1862 and that it came from 'the late Mr Thomas [sic]

Beckford's Collection at Fonthill'; a portrait of More is listed in the 1823 Fonthill Sale catalogue. Derived from the Frick Collection portrait of Cromwell.

See nos. 804–5.

820. The Dresden version of Holbein's Adoration of the Virgin and Child with the Meyer family. Wrongly described as of the More family in the eighteenth century.

See. p. 69.

821. Uffizi Gallery, Florence (40799). Called 'More by Holbein' in catalogues from 1863 to 1899; possibly of Sir Thomas Hoby.

See *Burlington Magazine*, LII (1928), p. 283.

822. Once in the Kirby collection, sold Christie's, 7 January 1899.

823. Sold at Christie's, 7 May 1864, lot 106.

824. In the Broke collection, Nacton, in 1797. Dated '1554, aet. 75'.

825. In the collection of the Duke of Newcastle, Clumber, *c.* 1857.

826. In the Shelley-Sidney collection, Penshurst, in 1775; later in the collection of Lord De L'isle and Dudley.

827. In the Wyndham collection, Petworth, *c.* 1857.

828. In the collection of the Duke of Devonshire, Hardwick Hall, *c.* 1825.

THE COLLAR OF SS

More's Collar of SS is one of the more constant elements in his portraiture: only the 'Galle' group of engravings fail to shew it at all, and the progressive deterioration of its likeness affords some guide to the order of the earlier engravings. It might well provide more evidence, but two immediate difficulties occur. The first is that there was no accepted or approved form of design for the collar, and one cannot therefore say that any of the variations shewn in different portraits is right or wrong; the second is that a number of variations do occur, even in the earliest representations, and it is impossible to trace any connection between them, or reason for them.

Livery collars first came in during the fourteenth century. Collars with broomcod emblem were given to friends or followers by Charles V and Charles VI of France; the rival houses of York and Lancaster early took them up, York wearing a collar made up of falcons and fetterlocks, and Lancaster of SS. The purpose of these chains was to indicate the allegiance or alliance of the wearer. The king of England might wear the broomcod collar of France as a gesture of amity: the effigy in Spratton Church of Sir John Swinford has a collar of SS which indicates his fealty to John of Gaunt. Swinford died in 1371, which effectively disposes of the only specious explanation put forward for the SS, that it stood for Henry IV's 'motto' *Soverayne*. In the fifteenth century, the giving of a collar came to be accepted as the accolade of the squire, as the tap of the sword on the shoulder was for knighthood. Under the Yorkist kings, the collar of SS was out of favour, but it was brought back by Henry VII, who further embellished it with the portcullis and, or as an alternative, the Tudor rose. While neither then nor now is it the mark of any particular office, its presentation was a mark of royal favour, its wearing of royal service.[1]

More may have received his chain as early as 1515 when he went on the embassy to Flanders; or in 1517, after the 'Evil May Day' riots in London and More's appearance representing the Pope in a case concerning the forfeiture of a ship before Wolsey and other judges in the Star Chamber, when according to Roper[2] he entered the King's service. He must have received it by 2 May 1521 when he became Under-Treasurer and was knighted. In the years that followed he wore it habitually, as we learn from Roper's account of the last day he wore it, 17 April 1534, when he was committed to the Tower.

Whom, as he was going thitherward, wearing, as he commonly did, a chain of gold about his neck, Sir Richard Cromwell, that had the charge of his conveyance thither, advised him to send home his chain to his wife, or to some of his children. 'Nay, Sir' quoth he, 'that I will not; for if I were taken in the field by my enemies, I would they should somewhat fare the better by me.'[3]

---

[1] For a fuller discussion, see A. H. Ormerod, 'The SS Collar', *The Catholic Lawyer*, vol. II (1956), pp. 123–30.

[2] *The Life of Sir Thomas More*, ed. E. V. Hitchcock, 1935, pp. 9–10.   [3] Ibid., pp. 74–5.

No doubt the chain was impounded with his gown, when he reached the Tower, but in this, we may be sure, it served a deeper purpose than More's rather strained reply may seem to indicate. More's jests were seldom idle, and the control he shewed before and after make it unlikely, as has been suggested,[1] that at this moment his high spirits had failed him. The fortitude and brilliance of his defence made his trial a legend throughout Europe; his famous last words on the scaffold 'that he died the King's good servant but God's first' contain the kernel of the matter. More was indicted for treason, and his defence, which nothing but the perjured evidence of Rich could shake, was that what he held upon his conscience was not and could not be treason against his king. So, when he refused to part with his chain until it was taken from him, he was saying, in effect, that no voluntary action of his would ever relieve him of his service to the king, which he maintained to the end.

His collar of SS, then, meant much to More; it is disappointing to find that an accurate depiction of it was not always achieved in his early portraits. The reason for this has been suggested: there was no accepted form for it. In early versions, the SS are found running consecutively (as in the Frick portrait), back to back, interlocked, and separated by other emblems. In the principal version which survives to the present day, that worn by the Lord Chief Justice, the SS are separated by a device of knots and roses. Other variants are worn by the kings-of-arms, the serjeants-at-arms, and the heralds; the Lord Mayor of London wears a fine example, given to the city in 1545 by Sir John Alen, thrice Lord Mayor. Small wonder, then, that some variation is found in the portraits of More. What is astonishing, however, is that the two versions which are certainly by Holbein, the Frick portrait and the Basel sketch, are different, the former showing a continuous SS on both sides of the clasp, and the latter a continuous chain of 'wrong reading' 22; furthermore, Locky's versions shew a further variation, with SS upon the right of the clasp and 22 on the left.

Later versions follow one or other of these variants, but they do not shew any regular or explicable order. The miniatures, whose resemblance to the group portrait has been noted, admittedly repeat the pattern of the Basel sketch, but Fowler's woodcut also has the continuous 22, where if it is indeed a reversed copy of a miniature, one would expect SS. Stapleton's engraving follows what is perhaps the authentic version and has SS. The corrupt version which first seems to appear in Wiericx's engraving approximates to SS, and the succession *Herω-ologia*–Elstracke–Valdor–Roper 1626 follows alternately 22 and SS as the figure faces right or left, thus confirming the order of copying. Wyngaerde suggests SS, but White who shews the chain in enlarged and exaggerated detail follows Locky. The Regi version and Vertue's engraving also enlarge the chain, but though they differ considerably from one another they both have the continuous SS. Altogether, it is a confused and unenlightening succession, and, unless or until some clearer notion of the original of the later engravings comes to light, it seems likely that it will remain so.

Nevertheless, its importance to the iconography of More should not be undervalued. It is the only ancillary to the portrait of More which is peculiar to him. The detail of cap, or tippet, or clothing may vary with the passage of time or from country to country, and the

[1] Christopher Hollis, *Sir Thomas More*, 1934, p. 249.

artist's interpretation is likely to be influenced by the fashion of his own time and place. But the chain seems always to have been known to be a special feature of the portraits of More; their authenticity can be measured to some extent by its presence or absence, and the accuracy with which it is depicted.[1] It is a detail which deserves the consideration of all who interest themselves in this subject.

[1] The curious exception to the rule is Wyngaerde's engraving. In it the detail of the chain is further from the authentic Holbein versions than anywhere else, and yet the engraver goes out of his way to inscribe his plate 'H. Holbeen in.'

'SUAVIUS OLET'

Exequias celebrate, aspargite floribus urnam,
Et tumulo castos aspiret laurus odores,
Sacrum laurigeri vatis complexa sepulchrum.
JOANNES SECUNDUS, *Naenia in morte Thomae Mori*

Mr J. B. Trapp has kindly pointed out that a more elaborate and finished version of the emblem on the bronze medallion and on the titlepage of Regi's *Vita* is to be found in Jacques Callot's *Vita Beatae Mariae Virginis matris Dei emblematibius delineata* (Paris, 1646). On folio 22 there is an engraving of a man cutting down a shrub, with the heading above:

POST FUNERA FRAGRAT
Sa bonne odeur s'accroist, après ces funerailles.

And below the following lines:

Dius Amor dum falce metit tua stamina, Virgo,
Balsameo tellus mersa liquore natat.

*

Le Baume que l'on fend d'une lame meutrière
Laisse escouler sa vie auecques sa liqueur
Et l'Amour, dont le traict touche la VIERGE au cœur,
Luy vient ouvrir le Ciel, en fermant sa paupière.

An emblematic work, such as Callot's *Life of the Virgin*, might well be expected to give a longer and more explicit description of its symbolic illustrations than is to be found in such casual manifestations as the medal and the title page. Yet the symbolism is not self-evidently clear, as the lines attached to Callot's plate reveal. It is surprising that no explanation of any sort—the addition of MART. to the inscription on the obverse of the medal, or a couplet on the titlepage—appears in either place to explain the emblem and its significance in the case of More. Moreover, there is the unlikely coincidence of the emblem appearing first in northern Europe in the sixteenth century and then in Italy at least a century later. It may perhaps be simply explained by the existence of a cast of the medal in Milan about 1675, but then how to account for the very different portrait of More on the frontispiece of Regi's work?

It seems possible therefore there was some work, written or engraved, which attached the symbol of the fragrance of the bough cut down to the untimely death of More, and that this work was the archetype of both medal and titlepage. But, if it exists, it has so far escaped discovery.

INDEX

Names of owners and locations of portraits, and titles of books, are indicated in italic type.

INDEX